JOSHUA
A True Servant Leader

OTHER BIBLICAL CHARACTER STUDIES BY WALTER C. KAISER, JR.

The Lives and Ministries of ELIJAH and ELISHA

ABRAHAM The Friend of God

Coming Soon

DAVID A Man After God's Own Heart

MOSES The Man Who Saw the Invisible God

JOSEPH From Prison to Palace

JOSHUA A True Servant Leader

NEHEMIAH The Wall Builder

SOLOMON The King with a Listening Heart

THE TWELVE The "Minor" Prophets Speak Today

JACOB The Journey from Jacob to Israel

ZECHARIAH The Quintessence of Old Testament Prophecy

DANIEL The Handwriting is on the Wall

RUTH The Moabite and the Providence of God

ESTHER God Preserves the Jewish Nation

JOSHUA
A True Servant Leader

Walter C. Kaiser, Jr.

Lederer Books
an imprint of
Messianic Jewish Publishers
Clarksville, MD 21029

Printed in the United States of America

Cover Design by Lisa Rubin,
Messianic Jewish Publishers
Graphic Design by Yvonne Vermillion,
MagicGraphix.com
Editor, George August Koch

1   2021
ISBN 9781951833145

Published by:
Lederer Books
An imprint of Messianic Jewish Publishers
6120 Day Long Lane
Clarksville, MD 21029

Distributed by:
Messianic Jewish Publishers & Resources
Order line: (800) 410-7367
lederer@messianicjewish.net
www.MessianicJewish.net

Dedication

To my grandson: Joshua Michael Christian Coley

"Be a good soldier of Christ Jesus"
2 Timothy 2:3

Introduction

Joshua: Moses' Aide

An Introduction to the Man and the Book

The story of Joshua is the narrative of a man who spent the first eighty years of his life in training to be a leader, and whose life would be marked by the life and skills of his mentor Moses. The book that bears his name describes how God gave his people Israel a territory in perpetuity at the eastern end of the Mediterranean Sea. The man Joshua, and the eponymous book, are of great importance— "for the history it records and for its internal teaching. But what makes the book of Joshua overwhelmingly important is that it stands as a bridge, a link between the Pentateuch (the writings of Moses) and the rest of Scripture. It is crucial for understanding the unity the Pentateuch has with all that follows it, including the New Testament."1

However, the story of Joshua begins in Exodus. Joshua enters the story of God's promise-plan for history shortly after Israel had crossed the Red Sea as they fled the Egyptians' ruthless oppression. A few days later, they came to Rephidim (Exodus 17), and murmuring broke out among the Jewish ranks. On God's command, Moses struck a rock, so water flowed copiously to the thirsty, complaining pilgrims. Soon after these events, the people of Israel were ambushed by the Amalekites, and suddenly Israel faced their first of many battles in the conquest of Canaan. It is at this point (Exodus 17:9) that Joshua appears for the first time. Moses instructed Joshua, his aide, to choose men to fight with him against this Amalekite host. Joshua experienced success in this initial

---

1 Francis A. Schaeffer, *Joshua and the Flow of Biblical History* (Downers Grove, IL: InterVarsity Press, 1975), 9.

contest, because as Moses sat on a rock watching him on the mountainside, Aaron and Hur upheld Moses' arms in prayer for this young man Joshua's success.

Later, Joshua went up on Mount Sinai with Moses and waited for him for forty days. When they descended to the foot of the mount, Joshua thought he heard the noise of war in the camp, but the more-experienced Moses corrected him, saying it was not the shout of victors, nor the cry of the vanquished, but the singing of the Israelites in the worship of the newly created idol, which turned out to be none other than the golden calf.

The next time Joshua comes to our notice is when he was with Moses and the newly selected seventy elders, who had been appointed to assist him. They experienced the power of the Holy Spirit in prophesying. Later, two of the seventy were not with the rest of the group, but the Spirit of God continued to rest upon them, and they kept on prophesying. When a young man informed Moses that two men, Eldad and Medad, were still prophesying, Joshua said, "Moses, my lord, stop them!" (Numbers 11:28) Moses gently rebuked Joshua, saying not to be jealous for Moses' reputation, for it would be wonderful if all the Lord's people were prophets and God would put his Spirit upon all of them (11:26–30).

Soon after, Joshua—who was called "Hoshea son of Nun"—was appointed a representative of the tribe of Ephraim to be one of the twelve spies to reconnoiter the land of Canaan. Moses gave Hoshea the name "Joshua" (Numbers 13:16), meaning "the LORD saves." In the Bible, the act of changing a name is very significant. For example, Abram's name became Abraham, Sarai to Sarah, Jacob to Israel, Simon to Cephas, Saul to Paul. As was true in all these cases, so too in Joshua's case this represented a major change in his life. Thus, as Joshua looked back on the victory God had given him over the Amalekites at Rephidim, God was beginning a new work in his life. It was also a testimony—to Moses' mentoring, to the Lord's inspiring Moses in this ministry to Joshua, and to Joshua's character and the fact that he would prefigure the saving work that would ultimately come to his people in the promise-plan of God.

Those forty days of touring as a spy the land of Israel must have been enormously enjoyable for Joshua. Imagine his joy as he visited many of the sites made memorable in the lives of his forefathers. Did Joshua take time to sit down under the oak tree as Abraham had? Did he examine the cave of Machpelah where five of his relatives were buried? Did he stop at Bethel, the place where the angels went up and down a ladder to heaven? How many more such places must have thrilled his heart and mind? But at the end of the forty-day search of the land, only he and Caleb gave a positive report and urged that Israel act in faith by going up to possess the land immediately! The two of them were later honored for their faith, but the other ten spies died with that whole generation. Interestingly enough, we hear nothing more of Joshua for a long time. He is first mentioned again 38 years later, just before Moses' death. In fact, God appointed him Moses' successor. Deuteronomy 31:23 says, "The LORD gave this command to Joshua son of Nun: 'Be strong and courageous, for you will bring the Israelites into the land I promised them on oath, and I myself will be with you.'"

A Successor and Leader Following Moses

It is true, of course, there are some leaders for whom it is almost impossible to find a comparable replacement! Sometimes this is because of an individual's extraordinary talent; sometimes it is because a people grow so accustomed to an individual's style that they cannot imagine another leader succeeding the one who departed.

The question for Joshua, then, was not whether he was a good fit to succeed Moses or not. Instead, the question was this: Had Joshua learned, during his eighty-some years of serving with Moses, that it is the Lord himself who shapes and makes leaders who will be his servants? This work of the Spirit of God can be seen in the formation of leaders.

It Is God Who Makes Leaders Great

This truth is clearly laid out in Joshua 3:7—

> And the LORD said to Joshua, "Today I will begin to exalt you in the eyes of all Israel, so that they may know I am with you as I was with Moses."

As if to stress this very same point, the text affirms that that is precisely what the Lord did for Joshua in Joshua 4:14—

> That day the LORD exalted Joshua in the sight of all Israel; and they revered him all the days of his life, just as they had revered Moses.

The Lord had instructed Moses, "Go up this mountain in the Abarim range and see the land I have given to the Israelites. After you have seen it, you too will be gathered to your people, as your brother Aaron was." Moses followed that piece of instruction and prayed: "May the LORD, the God of the spirits of mankind, appoint a man over this community to go out and come in before them, one who will lead them out and bring them in, so the LORD's people will not be like sheep without a shepherd" (Numbers 27:16–17).

That word from Moses was immediately followed by God's promise:

> "Take Joshua son of Nun, a man in whom is the Spirit, and lay your hand on him. Have him stand before Eleazar the priest and the entire congregation and commission him in their presence. Give him some of your authority so the whole Israelite community will obey him. He is to stand before Eleazar the priest, who will obtain decisions for him by inquiring of the Urim before the LORD. At his command he and the entire community of Israelites will go out, and at his command will come in." (Numbers 27:18–21)

It is significant to notice that Joshua was not exalted or raised to prominence by a press that fawned over him and set him up as an outstanding leader for their time. Instead, it was the Lord God who exalted Joshua. Joshua did not try to create his image and reputation in the eyes of the people; rather, he left that work up to the Lord himself.

It Is God Who Helps Leaders to Be Servant-Leaders

As Joshua began his service under Moses, he was merely an "aide" to Moses (Joshua 1:1). The importance of the name "Moses" for Joshua's years of service can be seen in the fact that Moses' name appears fifty-nine times in Joshua: eleven times in the first chapter alone, and another forty-eight times in the rest of the book. No wonder, then, that Joshua possessed the habit of being a "servant-leader" as Moses exhibited in his life.

The Lord promised Joshua, "As I was with Moses, so I will be with you. I will never leave you nor forsake you" (1:5b). As he did in Deuteronomy 31:23, the almighty Lord of creation encouraged Joshua:

> "Be strong and courageous, because you will lead these people to inherit the land I swore to their forefathers to give them. Be strong and very courageous. Be careful to obey all the law my servant Moses gave you; do not turn from it to the right or to the left, that you may be successful wherever you go. Do not let this Book of the Law depart from your mouth; meditate on it day and night, so that you may be careful to do everything written in it. Then you will be prosperous and successful. Have not I commanded you? Be strong and courageous. Do not be terrified; do not be discouraged, for the LORD your God will go with you wherever you go." (1:6–9)

At first, then, Joshua was merely a youthful page freely serving his master. But if we could trace any outstanding happening in his life that began to make the difference, and possibly marked a transition in his life, it had to be his decision to "be strong and courageous" and "careful to obey all the law my servant Moses gave you." This guide would never depart from his mouth; in fact, Joshua was to meditate on it day and night (1:7–9).

Moses was remembered especially as God's "servant." The first words of the book of Joshua herald this title: "After the death of Moses, the *servant* of the LORD," God announced to Joshua: "Moses my *servant* is dead" (1:1–2). He instructed Joshua, "Be careful to obey all the law my *servant* Moses gave you" (1:7). God reminded Joshua of Moses acting as his "servant" over and over again in this book (1:1–2, 7, 13–14; 8:31, 33; 9:24; 11:12, 15; 12:6, 8; 14:7; 18:7; 22:2, 4–5).

It Is God Who Makes Leaders by Reminding Them of the Past

Joshua was instructed to help the future generations by setting up "memorial stones" across the landscape. This was done so that when the children asked their parents and the older generation, "What do these stones mean?" (4:6, 21), they were to tell them that "these stones are to be memorials to the people of Israel forever" (4:7d).

The first place where one of these stones was erected was in Gilgal. After Israel had crossed the Jordan River, Joshua ordered twelve men to be chosen, one from each tribe, and they were to take up twelve stones from the middle of the Jordan, where the priests had stood as the Israelites passed over that river that had been up to flood stage. No sooner had the priests set foot on dry ground than the waters once again ran at flood stage (4:18). Thus, on the tenth day of the first month, the people went across the Jordan and camped at Gilgal, east of Jericho (4:19). There Joshua had the men set up the twelve stones they had taken from the Jordan River and gave these instructions to relay to their children, when they asked about the meaning of this pile of stones:

"Tell them, Israel crossed the Jordan on dry ground. For the LORD your God dried up the Jordan before you until you crossed over. The LORD your God did to the Jordan just what he had done to the Red Sea when he dried it up until we had crossed over. He did this so that all the peoples of the earth might know that the hand of the LORD is powerful and so that you might always fear the LORD your God." (4:22–24)

The next pile of stones actually came as a reminder that the word of the Lord was to be followed carefully and fully, or judgment would follow. Achan the son of Zerah stole some of the loot discovered at Jericho that had been devoted to destruction for the Lord himself. Therefore, when Israel attempted to conquer the next village, small Ai, they lost thirty-six men and were chased off in disgrace. When it was learned that Achan had violated the covenant of the Lord by taking some of the "doomed things" (7:1). (The Hebrew uses *herem*, meaning things that should be destroyed.) The nation of Israel then took Achan to the Valley of Achor, and there Israel stoned him and "heaped up a large pile of rocks, which remains to this day" (7:26).

Joshua was given a mighty victory over the five southern kings of the Amorites—Jerusalem, Hebron, Jarmuth, Lachish, and Eglon—as he pursued them along the road that goes up to Beth-Horon. There the Lord hurled down on the Amorites such huge hailstones that "more of them died from the hail than were killed by the swords of the Israelites" (10:11). The five kings hid in a cave at Makkedah, so Joshua commanded that large stones be rolled up to the mouth of the cave until he returned. When Joshua came back to the cave, he killed the kings and hung them on five trees until evening came. Then he threw their corpses into the cave where they had been hiding and closed the mouth of the cave with "large rocks, which are there to this day" (10:27).

It Is God Who Makes Leaders by Acting on Their Behalf

As the book of Joshua ticks off the cities and places where our Lord had dramatically intervened in fulfilling his promise to be with Joshua and the army of Israel as they conquered the land, we are given proof of the fact that he has indeed acted on behalf of this leader named Joshua. We need only to recall the names of places like Jericho, Ai, Gibeon, the cave of Makkedah, etc.

God made Joshua and Israel great again, after 400 years mostly of slavery in Egypt. Their "greatness" was not the result of their own skills, achievements, or character, for if mortals ever accomplish anything worth noting in their lives or history, it must come from God. God had promised Joshua that he would exalt him just as he had exalted Moses, and so he did.

Conclusions

1. Promotion to leadership comes neither from the east nor from the west, but from the Lord. Likewise, any honors and accomplishments are gifts from our Heavenly Father.
2. Our Lord is looking for leaders who are "servants"; he is not looking for those who are autocratic and self-seeking souls who long to make themselves rich, or for public adulation and praise.
3. Our Lord often places markers like a pile of stones along our pathways that are key reminders of who he is and what he has done for us. Can you think of any such markers in your own life?
4. Joshua was fine with serving as an aide to Moses for 80-some years of his life. If he had aspired to be a leader, he surely must have abandoned them and felt there was no chance that would happen after he got into his 50s.

Questions for Thought or Discussion

1. What is your opinion makes a leader and what goes along with his allowing us to declare him as great? Why are these criteria missing so often from current leaders?

2. Have you noticed how Joshua served for almost 80 years without demanding to be noticed or given any guarantee that he would be next in line? When did he learn that he would follow Moses as a leader? How scary must that have been for a man who was not viewed for all those years as a prominent person with recognized skills to be named suddenly by the Lord as the new leader?

3. How could the study and meditation on the word of God enable him to be a great leader?

4. Why were the Lord's words to Joshua to "be strong, be courageous" repeated to him several times? What was so unique to his situation that he specially needed those words?

5. God promised Joshua "prosperity" and "success." How could the Lord assure Moses this was more than just a nice wish for new leaders?

Lesson 1

Acting on the Promises of God

Joshua 1:1–18

The book of Joshua begins on a most solemn note: "Moses my servant is dead" (1:2a). But now it was time for the new man to take his first step as leader: "Now you and all these people, get ready to cross the Jordan River into the land I am about to give to them" (1:2b). The time had come for Joshua to take decisive action, for the bold step of possessing the land God had promised to Israel some 700 years ago was at hand! Here was an especially exciting moment, second in importance and significance only to an event that had occurred forty years ago, when their fathers had stood on the edge of the parting Red Sea, the walls of water rolling back to form an aisle between the mountainous waves as Pharaoh's chariots were closing in on Israel. But this was it; the hour had come, for the promise God had made to Abraham, Isaac, Jacob, and Moses was about to be fulfilled! Our Lord had not been in a hurry to fulfill his promises, yet neither had he forgotten what he had promised; it would now begin to come to pass!

Remember the Pledge of My Powerful Presence – 1:1–5

Verse 2 of this first chapter of Joshua begins with God's striking use of the introductory word "now." The old age of Moses had just ended, and now God's new revelation and promises were about to begin. The man God had chosen to initiate this new moment of his "now" was a man called "Joshua son of Nun." But "Nun" has no relation to the English word "none"; in fact, the Hebrew word "Nun" means "to sprout forth or continue"—the perfect name for the leader who was to follow Moses.

God's "now" continues for each generation. Consider what is written in Hebrews 13:5–6, which reads:

> "Keep your lives free from the love of money and be content with what you have, because God has said, 'Never will I leave you; never will I forsake you.' So, we say with confidence, 'The Lord is my helper; I will not be afraid. What can man do to me?'"

In this context, God's key promise to Joshua was the unmistakable gift of the land of Canaan (1:2–4, 6, 11, 15). This specific land could be described as bounded by these markers: on the north by the nation of Lebanon and the ponderous Mount Hermon; on the east by the Euphrates River; on the west by the Mediterranean Sea; and on the south by the Wadi el-Arish, which flowed into the Mediterranean Sea about 50 miles south of the Gaza Strip, but cut diagonally across the desert to the north end of the Gulf of Aqabah. The promise of the land had been one of the main declarations of our Lord during the Patriarchal Period.1 In fact, "land" is the fourth-most-frequently-used noun in the Old Testament!

Two things might well have caused some hesitation on the part of Joshua and the people to cross the Jordan. In the first place, the river was in its annual flood stage (3:15). Having overflown its banks and now flowing rapidly, crossing at this time was out of the question. In the second place, if Israel crossed the river and moved into the land of Canaan, it would be like throwing down the gauntlet to the Canaanites. It would be tantamount to making an open declaration of war and a challenge for the enemy to round up the various nations in that land to begin to fight Israel with all their might, whether they were ready or not.

But our Lord never gives impossible commands. And the very fact that the Living God had commanded the crossing was clear evidence that he was ready to make it happen! It is just such faith in God's power that makes the hardest tasks possible and successful.

---

[1] See Genesis 12:6–7; 13:14–15; 15:7, 18–21; 17:8; 24:7; 26:3–4; 28:13–14; 35:12; 48:3–4.

Was this not also true in the case of Columbus, who sailed the ocean in 1492, and who heard a divine voice to cross the uncharted waters of the Atlantic in his desire to bring natives of the distant shores to hear the message of God's grace and salvation? Was this not also the situation in the life of David Livingstone, who felt he was being called by God to strike into the heart of the African continent to throw open its doors to teaching and preaching the gospel?

Meditate Continuously on the Word of God – 1:6 –9

Three times in this opening chapter of Joshua, the Lord charges him to "be strong and courageous" (1:6, 7, 18). These words are very similar to those found in Deuteronomy 3:28; 31:7, 23—

> "But [you, Moses] commission Joshua, and encourage and strengthen him, for he will lead this people across and will cause them to inherit the land that you will see." (Deuteronomy 3:28, emphasis mine)

> Then Moses summoned Joshua and said to him in the presence of all Israel, "Be *strong* and *courageous*, for you must go with this people into the land that the LORD swore to your forefathers to give them, and you must divide it among them as their inheritance." (Deuteronomy 31:7, emphasis mine)

> The LORD gave this command to Joshua son of Nun: "Be *strong* and *courageous*, for I will bring the Israelites into the land I promised them on oath, and I myself will be with you." (Deuteronomy 31:23, emphasis mine)

The Lord knew Joshua would need courage, for the opposition he would face from the Canaanite kings would be awesome. He would also need courage to live personally according to the teaching of the word of God. Add to that his need for courage to walk with the Lord, who would lead him into unexpected places and ways.

Most important of all, Joshua was told: "Be careful to obey all the law my servant Moses gave you" (1:6). Especially for a leader who was to lead a busy life, the habit of meditating on the word of God was mandatory. This did not call for a cursory perusal of the book of the Law from time to time. For Joshua, and likewise in every age in the life of the people of God, there could be no prosperity or progress among God's people without the constant guidance of God's word. This word from God was like fresh manna, which was new every morning!

Think of men like George Mueller of Bristol, who read the entire Bible from start to finish over a hundred times, but never found it less fresh and helpful each time. When David Livingstone was detained at Manyuema, he read the Bible in full four times. Henry Stanley, the man who went to find Livingstone, read the entire Bible three times during the Emin Expedition.

Moses urged Joshua not to let this Book of the Law depart from his mouth (1:8). Earlier, Moses had taught Joshua and the people that men and women do not live by bread alone, but by every word that comes from the mouth of God (Deuteronomy 8:3). Therefore, Joshua was to talk about the word of God, contemplate the word of God, and do what the word of God said! Even though Joshua was thoroughly acquainted with Moses and all his faults and sins as well as his frequent times of excelling in obedience to the word, Joshua also knew immediately after the death of Moses that the five books he had written under the inspiration of the Holy Spirit were nothing less than the word of God. Joshua did not need to wait until word allegedly came in 90 C.E. from the Council of Jamnia that the five Torah books were part of the sacred Scriptures. No wonder, then, that Joshua was identified as "a man in whom is the Spirit" (Numbers 27:18).

Joshua was to delight in the word of God, as Psalm 1:2 urges. The word was to be the source of meditation day and night. If this man was to be the man God had called him to be, there would be nothing other than God's word as his primary delight.

Make Preparations to Receive the Promises of God – 1:10–11

God had spoken to Joshua, and now it was time for Joshua to speak to the people. He was to order his officers to go through the camp to tell the people to ready their supplies (1:11). These "supplies" seem to refer to the natural products of the country, for we read in another context, "The manna stopped the day after they ate this food from the land; there was no longer any manna for the Israelites, but that year they ate of the produce of Canaan" (5:12).

There would only be three more days left of the forty years of wandering in the wilderness. During those three days, Israel was to prepare themselves in a consecration not unlike the consecration and purification that had taken place at the foot of Mount Sinai (Exodus 19:10–11). All impurities found among the people's hearts and lives was to be removed if they were to get properly ready for entering and walking in the land with their Lord.

To be sure, all of life was to be lived to the glory of God, but not everything in life was sacred. So, in these three days of preparation, ordinary pleasures were not to be indulged in (1 Samuel 21:4–5).

At the end of the three days, Israel, under Joshua's leadership, was to cross the Jordan, enter, and take possession of the land the Lord their God was giving them (1:11). The word the Lord used to "possess" the land had an archaic meaning of "to tread on [it]," as one would "tread on" the grapes to extract the juice. Hence, the word to "tread" on the land (or "possess" it) is to conquer it (see Micah 5:5–6; Deuteronomy 11:24–25). Ultimately, "Your seed shall *possess* [*yarash*] the nations" (Isaiah 54:3).

Unite with God's People to Finish the Task – 1:12–18

This command must be read and understood against the background of Numbers 32, for after Israel had defeated the Transjordanian kings Sihon and Og, two and a half tribes—the

Reubenites, Gadites and the half-tribe of Manasseh—requested they be given that land as their possession. But this infuriated Moses; as he saw it, these two-and-a-half tribes were opting out of the war of driving out the Canaanites. This would have a bad effect on the other tribes, like what Israel had experienced in the bad report of ten of the twelve spies who went up to reconnoiter the land (Numbers 32:14–15).

However, the two-and-a-half tribes responded by affirming that they were ready to arm themselves and to go ahead of their kin and brethren to fight with them in opening up the land. Only after the battle for Canaan had been won would they return (Numbers 32:17–18).

Joshua obtained from them a promise of loyalty, which seemed to be beyond anything they had ever given Moses. It was a matter of great concern to Moses that the people so habitually complained to and blamed him for the hardships they had been given for their sins in the wilderness. It was the people's unwillingness to trust him, even after all he had sacrificed for them, that makes the contrast here so strong.

The unanimity of the people in their loyalty to Joshua is of special note. There does not appear to be one dissenting vote in this outburst of loyalty to God's servant Joshua. He did not have to face a rebellious Korah, Dathan, or Abiram as Moses been plagued with. Joshua was therefore blessed of the Lord in this regard.

God promised "rest" (Hebrew *menuchah*) to his people Israel after they had finished the work of cleansing the land of the Canaanites. There was both a physical as well as a spiritual side to this rest. Rest is a gift that comes from God and is received by faith in the Lord, on whom we are to cast all our cares and concerns (see Matthew 11:28).

This rest is also a picture of the eternal Sabbath rest that awaits God's people (Hebrews 4:9). In this instance, it is a delight to see the people's obedience, compared to their rebellion in the wilderness

(Exodus 15:25; Numbers 19:2–3; Deuteronomy 9:22–23). It is, however, somewhat surprising to hear the people of Israel say: "Just as we fully obeyed Moses, so we will obey you!" (1:17) Their one desire was this: "Only may the LORD your God be with you as he was with Moses. Whoever rebels against your word and does not obey your words, whatever you may command them, will be put to death. Only be strong and courageous" (17b–18).

Conclusions

1. Three times this first chapter of Joshua stressed that Joshua was to "be strong and courageous." Both strength and courage were needed, and the Lord would gift him with them.
2. Israel was to enter the land at the most unthinkable time: the river at its flood stage, and in the springtime, when armies traditionally went forth to war.
3. Just as Moses experienced the presence of God, so the Lord would never leave or forsake Joshua. He had seen how many times God had intervened on Moses' behalf in a wonderful and miraculous way, which is why he took special comfort in this word of assurance.
4. The word of God would be the source of Joshua's success. Therefore, Joshua was to make it his object of meditation day and night.
5. The promise of the gift of the land is central to this passage and an important part of the promise-plan of God.

Questions for Thought or Discussion

1. How does one rise to accept the role of leader after that person has served 80 years as an aide and a servant to the main man?
2. How does Israel's present occupying of the land fit with the boundaries noted in this text? Why is there this disparity?

3. How can Bible reading, study, and meditation actually make a person prosperous and successful? What is the extent and the manifestation of that success and prosperity?

4. How certain was Joshua that the two-and-a-half tribes, who had built pens for their animals on the eastern side of the Jordan, would leave their wives and children and go with the other tribes to fight for the land of Canaan? What if they rebelled?

5. How would you describe the promise of God's rest to Israel? Is that same rest still available today?

Lesson 2

Confessing God's Control Over All

Joshua 2:1–24

J oshua had been promised "strength" and "courage" for the task ahead of him. Thus, it was not a long time after that promise that both he and the people of Israel would be called upon to practice that very same courage and to demonstrate that strength sent from God above! As part of the plan to now drive out the seven nations of Canaan from the land they had polluted with their sins, Joshua would begin by engaging the skills of two men who were ready for the duty of spying and risk to their lives. Joshua himself, in an earlier day, had been one of the twelve spies sent out to reconnoiter the land, so he knew some of the risks and dangers these two men must face, if not endure.

In His Providential Preparation of All Our Ways – 2:1–7

From the form of the Hebrew verb translated as "had sent," it would seem Joshua sent his two spies on the morning on the same day on which Israel's leader Joshua announced that in three days the nation would move out of their encampment at Shittim to cross the Jordan River. These two spies were ordered to go to Jericho. After fording the Jordan—presumably by swimming across it at flood stage—they came to the city of Jericho that same afternoon after traversing about five miles from the river. But after they got there, they were alarmed that the king of Jericho had learned of their presence and ordered a search for them, so that evening, Rahab the harlot helped them flee to the mountains west of town. There they remained, as Rahab had counseled them, until the next day, leaving that area on the third day to return to link up with Israel on the east side of the Jordan, who were ready to make the momentous crossing of the river. Verse 22 says the two spies stayed in the mountains for three days.

The king of Jericho knew where to go when he heard of foreigners had come to his city, for in v. 3 he sent a message to Rahab: "Bring out the men who came to you and entered your house, because they have come to spy out the whole land." This immediately raises a moral question for modern believers: Why did the spies go to a harlot's house? The answer shouldn't be difficult, for Rahab's place functioned not only as a possible house of prostitution, but it must have also been a sort of bar or a tavern where people who were seeking cover could easily "get lost" and "get news" about what was going on. Rahab must have been in the king's employ as his eyes and ears to learn any possible national intelligence as she listened to the talk of the customers, especially as they got drunk and their tongues moved more easily. Rahab's place, then, was a place where people were coming and going. There is no suggestion in the text, however, that the Israelite spies went there for any immoral purposes. Besides, almost from the moment they arrived, they were too busy trying to avoid discovery!

How could Rahab, a Gentile, pagan woman, have expressed such strong faith in the Lord and yet been a "harlot" (and perhaps the owner of a tavern)? The answer is that often the light that guides changes in some of these areas comes to believers gradually over a period of time, just as John Newton could write a hymn "Amazing Grace" after he received Christ into his heart, but still continue for some time after his conversion to carry cargoes of slaves in his ship.

Now Rahab had taken the two spies and she had hidden them up on her roof (v. 4). Therefore, when she was ordered by the king of Jericho to "bring out the men" (v. 3), she responded:

> "Yes, the men came to me, but I did not know where they had come from. At dusk, when it was time to close the city gate, the men left. I don't know which way they went. Go after them quickly. You may catch up with them." (4b–5)

She was trying to throw the king off their trail, for in the meantime, she had hidden them under the stalks of flax she had laid out on the roof (v. 6). There is no question that the Bible gave Rahab high praise for her faith in the Lord (Hebrews 11:31), and for giving lodging to the spies and sending them off in a different direction than those seeking them (James 2:25).

Rahab should not be assigned guilt or fault for abandoning her Canaanite people. She honored the Lord more than she feared the king of Jericho. Truth-telling is a covenantal responsibility, but this does not mean we should surrender innocent lives to the enemy (such as the two spies) just because an army, police force, or a king demands it. There are times for legitimate civil disobedience; this is because the law of God takes priority. Accordingly, Rahab was justified in hiding the spies on her roof among the drying flax-stems.

In His Appeal to the Nations Through His Acts in History – 2:8–14

Rahab turned out to be very helpful to the spies, for not only did she give them shelter, but she also gave them valuable information which became the heart of what the two of them would report to Joshua. This was her message to them:

> "I know that the LORD has given this land to you and that a great fear has fallen on us, so that all who live in this country are melting with fear because of you. We have heard how the LORD dried up the water of the Red Sea for you when you came out of Egypt, and what you did to Sihon and Og, the two kings of the Amorites east of the Jordan, whom you completely destroyed. When we heard it, our hearts melted and everyone's courage failed because of you, for the LORD your God is God in heaven above and on the earth below." (2:9–11)

Rahab's testimony is really remarkable. This Canaanite, who lived across the Jordan and who met these two men, was no ordinary person. Rahab made a most-explicit confession of her faith in *ADONAI*—not only as the God of the Hebrews, but as the only God in both heaven and earth! The Lord God was the only God that existed in heaven above and on the earth beneath—Baal and Ashtoreth were nowhere to be seen or heard! This confession alone must have run directly counter to all she had been taught to observe from her youth onward; against all that her neighbors had believed and all her priests and handlers had urged her to observe.

She was no great philosopher or teacher, but when she had heard, along with her fellow citizens of Jericho, how the Lord had dried up the Red Sea when Israel came out of Egypt and what Israel had done in their conquest with the kings of Sihon and Og, she did not need any additional arguments, for she knew no one can have such extraordinary effects without equally great causes. Rahab was a whole lot smarter than many of those who hold to modern unbelief—despite all of modernity's pretensions to mastering philosophy or science, it has over the centuries constantly accepted effects without naming an adequate cause.[1]

In His Deliverance of All Who Trust in Him – 2:15–24

Rahab let the two spies down from the window in her house, which was built in the wall of the city of Jericho, by a rope, also called a "scarlet cord" (vv. 15, 21). No doubt this window was the very same one through which the bundles of flax had just recently been pulled up on her roof. From this flax, the poor and lower-middle-class of Jericho produced linen garments for city's priests and upper class. In fact, 1 Chronicles 4:21 mentions those in Israel who were part of "the families of the house of linen workers."

Some commentators have emphatically argued that the "scarlet cord" was an emblem of the blood of Yeshua by which sinners are

---

1 See a similar comment by William Garden Blaikie, *The Book of Joshua* (Minneapolis: Klock & Klock Christian Publishers, 1978), 87.

redeemed. This line of thinking can be seen as far back as Clement of Rome, an early Church father. But commentators should not be dogmatic about such a significance since the Bible does not explicitly make this connection. Instead, why not regard this scarlet cord as a marker of Rahab's house, which thereby put her under as much protection as did the Paschal Lamb, whose blood was shed at the Passover in Egypt.

The men instructed Rahab to bring her father and mother and all her family into her house (v. 18). They were to quarantine themselves inside and not go out into the street, nor tell what the spies had been doing there, otherwise the men would not be responsible for them with their lives, for if they violated these terms, then the two spies would be released from the oath they had made with Rahab (vv. 19–20). This plan was agreed to by all.

The spies left Rahab's house that night and went into the hills and stayed there until three days had expired (v. 22). Then the two men started back to meet and report to Joshua (v. 23a). They forded the river once again and met Joshua, to whom they told all they had learned in their mission (vv. 23–24). The two men's summary was this: "The LORD has surely given the whole land into our hands; all the people are melting in fear because of us" (v. 24).

Surprisingly, the spies did not give Joshua any ideas as to how Jericho might be taken; however, they gave him something immensely better: God's outstretched hand was so powerful that the inhabitants of the whole country—not just Jericho alone—which they were about to take over, was completely paralyzed on account of what God has done! These two spies were not like the previous ten spies, who had been sent out as a party of twelve, but who came back after surveying the land with a strong dissent from Caleb and Joshua's minority report. On the contrary, these two spies looked upon the conquest of the land as one which had already been conquered, for "the LORD has surely given the whole land into our hands."

This study cannot end without noting that Rahab, despite her ill reputation prior to her salvation, is found along with three other women (Tamar, Ruth, Bathsheba) in the narrative about when the tabernacle was raised in the days of Moses, which would be about 39 years before the events of this crossing of the Jordan. In that ceremony with the tabernacle, twelve princes were selected, one from each tribe, to make a special offering. The first one from the tribe of Judah was Nahshon, the son of Amminadab. Nahshon's son was Salmon, the man who later married Rahab. Not only did this harlot become a believer, but she became the wife of a prince in Judah! How is that for the grace of God!

Salmon and Rahab had a son named Obed (see Ruth 4:20–22), who in turn begat Jesse, the father of David (Matthew 1:4–6). David became the head of the line of Yeshua, our Lord.

According to Joshua 6:25, Rahab continued to dwell in Israel even up to the time the book was written. She stood among the people of God not as an unclean harlot, but under the blood of the Son of God, who loved her and gave himself for her. If some think it is not fitting for her to be the ancestress of Christ, then the question should be asked: Are *we* any more worthy to have been given the grace of God?

Conclusions

1. Rahab is a model for us of hope and terrific evidence of the grace of God. She who was at the bottom of the social scale found out that indeed, "harlots will go into the kingdom of God before you," as Yeshua taught (Matthew 21:31).
2. Rahab acted on the little she knew, but she did act—and so should we.
3. We too should confess that there is no match that can compete with our Sovereign Lord.
4. Is it not true that our Lord has often prepared the way for us in our lives?

5. Is it not God's plan to bless each one of us who believe with his gift of salvation that he has made available to us through the line of the people of Israel and particularly in the line of King David, among whose line can be found Rahab?

Questions for Thought or Discussion

1. Rahab's confession of faith begins with the confident assertion of "I know." How could she be so certain of her salvation with such a short supply of information?
2. Contrast Rahab with the man Achan in these areas:
3. In their economic and social status.
4. How each helped or hindered in the conquest for the land.
5. In how each carried out the covenant they had made at the time.
6. In the effect they had on their families.
7. How is Rahab a woman of exemplary faith? What roles do Hebrews 11:31 and James 2:25 play in this evaluation?
8. Name the four women in Matthew's genealogy of Yeshua and relate the negative aspect we know of each. Would this not detract from Yeshua's reputation and high office?

Lesson 3

Extolling the Greatness of Our God

Joshua 3:1–4:24

The description of what happened as Israel left Shittim in Jordan to go to Gilgal in Canaan is at the heart of Joshua 3–4, and it stands as one of the key passages to show us Israel's understanding of her mission. The nation's previous journey had traced her route, which began in Egypt at the area called Goshen, near Rameses (Exodus 12:37) and continued for the next forty years to the banks of the Jordan. In Numbers, the Hebrew verb *nasa'* appears 89 times; the word means Israel "journeyed" or "set out," for her task was one of "going onward" (Exodus 40:36–37). But in Joshua, this verb occurs only three times: once when Joshua and the congregation left Shittim (Joshua 3:1) and twice when they "set out" from the east bank to cross the Jordan (3:3, 14).

From that point onward in Joshua, however, the Hebrew verb `abar, meaning to "cross over," is used 21 times as Israel crossed the Jordan. Thus, the text emphasized a most-decisive moment in Israel's history! `Abar implies the crossing over of a physical boundary (such as a river or valley) or a national one. Accordingly, Israel's "crossing over" meant not only an escape from the desert and the arduous journey through the wilderness, but the crossing of the Jordan meant an entry into a new kind of life in the Land of Promise. To be sure, the entrance into the land of Canaan was not like a return all the way back to the Garden of Eden, where there would no longer be any problems, or a place identified within the kingdom of God; no, that was not what this crossing was about. Instead, it was a place where men and women could learn not only the discipline of hard work, but also the joy of success after years in the wilderness.

One other emphasis in these two chapters deserves our attention: how the Ark of God is the centerpiece of Joshua 3–4, being mentioned some 15 or more times. But let us turn to the text itself.

Remember How the Presence of God Seen with the Ark of the Covenant Encouraged Us – 3:1–6

Joshua and the Israelites camped by the Jordan, and after three days, they were told that when they saw the Levitical priests carrying the Ark of the Lord across the river, they were to follow it but not go near it (3:1–4). The simplest way to describe this holy object from the tabernacle was to simply call it the "ark" (3:15; 4:10). But it was also known as the "Ark of the LORD" (4:11) or the "Ark of the LORD your God" (4:5). In Psalm 80:1 and 99:1, it was clear that the Ark was noted for being a throne for the Living and Invisible God, who was seen as "seated" between the cherubim, which were represented as winged lions with human faces and were placed on either side of the ark (Exodus 25:18–19). However, along with these other names, the most-frequent way to refer to the Ark is "the Ark of the Covenant" (3:3, 6, 8, 11, 14, 17; 4:7, 9, 18).

Therefore, as the Levites carried the Ark as the people journeyed, it symbolized the conviction that God went along with them, guiding and protecting them as they traversed the wilderness. The distinctiveness of this concept can be seen in Exodus 33:16, where Moses asked the Lord, "How will anyone know that you are pleased with me and with your people unless you go with us? What else will distinguish me and your people from all the other people on the face of the earth?"

A "pillar of cloud by day and fire by night" had accompanied and led Israel through the wilderness for forty years. Now, from the throne above the Ark, God spoke to Moses (Exodus 25:22; Numbers 7:89). The cover on the Ark was also the place of Atonement, for on that cover the blood of Atonement was sprinkled (Leviticus 16:15) once every year on Yom Kippur.

Indeed, it was the Apostle Paul who called Yeshua the true "mercy-seat," which was another name for the Ark. *In this sense, then,* the Ark set forth a public proclamation of God's presence and power in the Atonement of his Son. Thus Yeshua "tabernacles" among his people (John 1:14) and is reconciled to them (2 Corinthians 5:19).

The Israelites were instructed to keep their distance from the Ark, about a thousand yards, as they crossed over the Jordan so all could see the works of God as the waters parted and the way was opened for the nation to cross over the Jordan River. This was not "social distancing" but "divine distancing"!

The Ark also taught the holiness of God (3:5). The people were told to "consecrate themselves" as was demanded for a special preparation to meet God. Such preparation might include washing one's clothes, abstaining from sexual relations and the like. But there were inward acts as well, such as confessing of one's sins and an attitude of reverential awe for the majesty and distinctiveness of God.

This raises the question as to whether we in our day are sufficiently impressed with the greatness of our God and his grandeur in our public worship. All of this takes preparation before we enter the public worship of God, or at the very least, offer a prayer of confession of our sin and join in the adoration of our God when we first take our seat in his house. Our Lord calls us to recognize his presence and holiness as part of our worship in his house. Only as we follow such a practice is our Lord able to show us his way and to "do any amazing things among us."

Remember How God's Leader Was Honored Among Us – 3:7–8; 4:14

God promised Joshua, "Today I will begin to exalt you in the eyes of all Israel, so that they may know I am with you as I was with Moses" (v. 7). This was crucial; imagine the jitters among the people as they faced two awesome events at the same time: the transition in leadership from Moses to Joshua, and the conquest of the entire country they were to inhabit after conquering it! So, it was important that the people knew Joshua had the seal of God's approval and would be competent to lead an inexperienced new nation unfamiliar with firsthand participation in fighting or statesmanship.

God would authenticate Joshua as leader as he showed his own miracle-working power on behalf of his new leader and his people Israel. It would be the fact that God would be present with his people and his leader that would make the difference for any and all who were timid or deeply concerned over the future of Israel.

Likewise, Hebrews 13:7 clearly teaches the following actions that the believing body is to take regarding their leaders: "Remember your leaders who spoke the word of God to you. Consider the outcome of their way of life and imitate their faith."

Along with that same teaching on respect and following one's leader was another Scripture from that same context, Hebrews 13:17: "Obey your leaders and submit to their authority. They keep watch over you as men who must give an account [to the LORD]. Obey them so that their work will be a joy, not a burden, for that would be of no advantage to you."

With that instruction completed, Joshua instructed the priests who carried the Ark of the Covenant to proceed into the riverbed. At precisely the point when their feet reached the edge of the Jordan's waters, they were to keep going (3:8). This would be another instance where trust in the power of the word of the Lord would be rewarded by his action.

Remember How God's Hand Provided for Us – 3:9–17; 4:14

Joshua continued to teach Israel how they were to act in this new situation (3:9). Right from the start of the conquest of the land, Joshua told Israel how they would know the Living God was among them. He would be the One who would drive out the seven pagan nations in the land that had been promised to Israel (3:10). Over the idols that made up the gods and goddesses in the land, who turned out to be "nothings" and lifeless (Deuteronomy 32:21; Jeremiah 8:19, 14:22; Psalm 31:7), Israel's God was the "living God" (3:10). He was alive and active in rescuing Israel, and this could be seen by the way he tamed the swollen Jordan at that very moment!

The Israelites might have feared that the time God had chosen for them to cross the Jordan was highly inauspicious, for the river had not only overflowed its banks, but it had added many additional feet of water over the banks of the land that spread out from the shore of the river, covering several miles of land.

At the same moment that Israel began to cross the river in faith, the Lord "cut off" the "waters flowing downstream" and "stood [them] up in a heap" (3:13). Interestingly, this damming up occurred in the "town of Adam" (v. 16) (modern name Tell ed-Damiyeh). Modern records attest that several landslides in 1267, 1906 and 1927 C.E. stopped the water from flowing downstream there. God's message to Israel, then, was this: If he could dry up a flooded, swollen river until all Israel passed over it, he could just as easily repel the swarms of hostile Canaanites who had to be driven out of the land. Likewise, God did not hold back his Son for our redemption, but he freely gave us all things needed for out salvation (see Romans 8:32).

The priests marched into the dried-up Jordan and stood there on dry ground in the middle of the river until the whole nation had gone across the river and stood on dry ground on the other side of the Jordan (3:17).

Remember How God's Signs Reminded Us of His Greatness —4:1–24

The same twelve men, who each represented one of the twelve tribes of Israel (3:12), are now addressed in more detail in 4:2. They were each to take as large a stone as they could carry from the place where the feet of priests stood, to the place where they would lodge for night, at Gilgal. In fact, however, they were to make two sets of stones to be raised as memorials for future generations. One pile of stones was to be set up at the place of their first encampment in the new land they were to conquer, at the site named Gilgal; the second pile of twelve stones was to be located in the bed of the river, exactly where the priests had stood holding the Ark as the nation of Israel crossed over (4:8–9).

These two piles of stones were to be a "sign" in their midst (4:6). Such a sign would be left as a memorial. This act was not new in Israel; Jacob had set up a pillar when he was at Bethel in Genesis 28:18. In his dream he had seen a stairway going from earth to heaven. It was the occasion when he was told, "I am with you and will watch over you (Genesis 28:15). Jacob set up another stone marker as a memorial sign in 35:14.

Special emphasis was placed on each of these piles of twelve stones, for it was anticipated that one day their children would ask the obvious question: "What is the meaning of these stones?" (4:6, 21) This would become a teaching moment, for when that question was asked, the parents and leaders were to tell them:

> "Israel crossed the Jordan on dry ground. For the LORD your God dried up the Jordan before you until they had crossed over. The LORD your God did to the Jordan just what he had done to the Red Sea when he dried it up before us until we had crossed over. He did this so that all the people of earth might know that the hand of the LORD is powerful and so that you might always fear the LORD your God. (4:22–24)

This was an ideal time for teaching children, including reciting the works of God, giving him glory for what he had done, and reminding future generations that they too should give him glory, showing they were thankful for what God had done for their ancestors, and therefore showing that their own generation had showed the proper obedience to such an awesome and powerful

God! The point was that what God had done was not only for the benefit of Israel, but so the whole world would see his hand powerfully at work for all mortals! (4:18, 24)

It was the tenth day of the first month that Israel crossed over the Jordan and camped their first night at Gilgal (4:19). It had also been the day when the paschal lamb had been set aside in Egypt (Exodus 12:2–3). This day marked the completion of Israel's redemption from Egypt! This was the day that the Lord had made for all in that nation to be glad and to rejoice in it (Psalm 118:24). Another of God's great works was now finished!

Conclusions

1. On this tenth day of the first month, our Lord finished what he had promised to Moses and Israel forty years ago (Psalm 118:24). Let us be glad and rejoice in that work!

2. No wonder Israel was told to set up two sites of the twelve memorial stones, both taken from the riverbed of the Jordan and at the site of the first night of camping in the land of Israel at Gilgal. These were real Ebenezer stones— "stones of remembrance"!

3. So prominent was the promise of the presence of the Lord that the priests carried the Ark of the Covenant into the middle of the dried-up stream of the Jordan to hold the waters back until everyone had successfully crossed over.

4. These actions by the Lord were so that Israel and the nations of the world might know that the "Living God" was among his people Israel and it was he who would drive out the seven pagan nations, whose cup of iniquity had now in the last 400 years risen and flowed over its rim (3:9; Genesis 15:13).

5. People are starving to witness the "Majesty of God." The Latin word for "majesty" means "greatness." On the mount of Transfiguration, Peter said: "We were eyewitnesses of [Yeshua's] majesty."

Questions for Thought or Discussion

1. If the greatest enemy of our faith is the sin of forgetfulness, what can a believer do to best overcome such a tragic response in the lives of those who claim to follow the Lord, especially after seeing a lifetime of the works of God on our behalf? (See Deuteronomy 8.)

2. What were the advantages and disadvantages of crossing the Jordan River in the springtime? Why did the Lord choose the spring to take Israel across the river?

3. What boundaries and general rules does our Lord set regarding our respect for our leaders? Why is it true that in opposing those leaders, we are also opposing God? How broadly does this principle extend—to a marriage? A congregation? Business relations? National leaders?

4. What are some of the memorial stones you have set up in your own life that mark distinctive moments when God met you or intervened on your behalf?

Lesson 4

Divine Intervention on Our Behalf

Joshua 5:1–6:5

News about the miraculous workings of our Lord soon spread to all the Amorite kings west of the Jordan River in Canaan and to all the Canaanite kings along the coast of the Mediterranean Sea (5:1). They heard how God dried up the Jordan at the time of the spring floods so Israel could cross over. They heard of the defeat of the Transjordanian kings Sihon and Og. These reports hit home for these pagan countries, and Israel's enemies lost the courage to fight. A deep, disheartening mood settled over the seven nations currently occupying the land God had given for Israel to possess. Nevertheless, the call to repent went out to these kings and nations, just as it had gone out to the people living in Jericho. Still, the call to repent went out to these kings and nations. God's invitation to be saved was universal.

Such an invitation has frequently been offered by our Lord over the centuries. For example, consider what happened in the United States, at the time of the great revival of 1857–1860, just prior to the Civil War. It began Wednesday, September 23, 1857, when a tall, middle-aged man, a former merchant named Jeremiah Lanphier, waited patiently in the eighty-year-old Dutch North Church at Fulton and Williams Street in New York City for anyone to join him from noon to one in prayer for revival. Lanphier had distributed thousands of handbills announcing this meeting, inviting those working in New York City to join him in earnest prayer for nationwide repentance and revival. At half-past twelve, one man showed up, followed by a few others at the quarter-hour until there were a total of six by 1:00

P.M. That was the total who had joined Jeremiah Lanphier for his first time of prayer for the nation's revival!

The second week, a total of twenty persons showed up. By the third week, there were forty. The very next week, the fourth week, on October 4, 1857, the U.S. faced a staggering financial panic as the banks of the nation closed, enormous numbers of jobs were lost, and families suffered. Despite this terrifying economic crash, Lanphier continued his noon gatherings for what would be known as the Fulton Street Prayer Meetings, or the Prayer Revival of 1857–58. Meanwhile, the numbers continued to grow, and after five months, 10,000 businesspersons (of a population of 800,000 New Yorkers) gathered for prayer. Out of this movement grew some twenty other groups. They formed elsewhere in the city and then spread across America, with numerous accounts of conversions and real repentance among believers being noticed by people everywhere.

God had accredited his servant Lanphier with such success in his call to prayer that in a short time, the whole world began to hear that God's power was mightily working in the lives of many, and that the Living God was dramatically operative among them in this time of urgent need and economic collapse!

In like manner, here in the book of Joshua, God prepared his leader Joshua and his people Israel and blessed them with a revival, demonstrated by the mighty power and presence of the Living God to all the surrounding nations that witnessed what God was doing for his own people.

The Effect of the Spectacular Crossing of the Jordan on the Amorite and Canaanite Nations – 5:1

Psalm 114 is devoted entirely to God's victory over the Red Sea and the Jordan River as Israel crossed over both on dry land. Verse 5 asks, "[What ails you], O sea, that you flood, O Jordan that you turned back." Likewise, Isaiah 51:9-11 made a similar point when it too declared:

"The song of the arm of the LORD when he dried up the waters making a way for the redeemed to pass over."

Meanwhile, others pictured the Jordan as a symbol of death, as exhibited by Welsh hymnist William Williams' (1717–1791) hymn "Guide Me, O Thou Great Redeemer." The lyrics read, in part:

When I tread the verge of Jordan,
Bid my anxious fears subside;
Death of death, and hell's destruction,
Land me safe on Canaan's side.

It is safer, however, to picture the Jordan as the last in a series of stages of moving from Egypt to the Promised Land. A better way to view this crossing of the Jordan River is to notice the importance of God's work in making this crossing possible. Again, as Joshua 5:1 says of the Amorite and Canaanite kings, "their hearts melted" when they heard how God had dried up the river. No longer did the kings have the courage to fight Israel. But let us not forget that through these events God was also calling the Amorite and Canaanite nations to turn to him for salvation, just as much as he had called in those former days to the Egyptians to acknowledge that he alone was the only true God and Lord over all powers and authorities.

We can be sure that the Amorite and Canaanite kings and people did not believe the drying up of the Jordan was just a stroke of luck or extraordinary coincidence Israel had experienced, as some liberal theologians claim. It was a mighty act of the miracle-working God who exceeded everything and anything the pagan gods and goddesses had ever done for those nations that opposed God. In fact, Israel celebrated these two great events to the glory of his name. Psalm 66:6 sang this note of praise: "[The LORD] turned the sea into dry land, [and] men passed through the river on foot!" Praise the name of our awesome God!

The Effect of the Act of Circumcision on Removing Israel's Reproach – 5:2–9

When Israel had crossing the river, they came to Gilgal—which, significantly enough, means "rolling away"; it was at that site that all who had been born during Israel's forty-year march through the desert were circumcised. The Lord commanded that the men of Israel should be circumcised before entering into the conquest of the land. In some ways, this was risky, for the men who had gone through the rite would need three days before they could once again take up the normal tasks of life, much less act as warriors in the land! If the hostile Canaanite nations had chosen to attack Israel immediately, they would have been unprepared for battle. But thanks be to God, the enemy did not strike immediately.

But in carrying out the rite of circumcision, the Lord told Joshua, "I have rolled away the reproach [Hebrew *herpah*] of Egypt from you" (5:9). The "reproach" was this: Israel had been the objects of humiliation, the recipients of disgrace and grave insults as they were forced by Pharaoh's labor bosses to manufacture as many bricks as possible each day. But it was not just Egypt that had reproached Israel; Zephaniah 2:8–9 points out that "[God] had heard the insults of Moab and the taunts of the Ammonites who insulted my people [Israel] and made threats against their land."

Israel needed a "circumcised heart" much more desperately than she needed a circumcision of the flesh; it was a spiritual cutting-away that would open the heart to belief in the word of the Lord and the obedience that went with it. During the wilderness wanderings, Moses warned that what was needed was "circumcision ... of the foreskin of [your] hearts" (Deuteronomy 10:16) in place of stubbornness and disobedience. Deuteronomy 30:6 said: "And the LORD your God will circumcise your heart ... to love the LORD your God with all your heart, with all your soul, that you may live." The prophet Jeremiah taught the same truth, "for all the house of Israel are uncircumcised in the heart" (Jeremiah 4:4, 9:26). Moreover, "Uncircumcised ears made it impossible to hear, leaving the people to scorn even the word of the LORD" (6:10).

The Apostle Paul also agrees, teaching that circumcision became uncircumcision through disobedience. This was because circumcision was a matter of the heart (Romans 2:25, 29). It did two things: It marked a person as Jewish, and it also marked one with the spiritual side of circumcision. But it is important to note that just because one generation disbelieved the promise of God and his oath, that did not negate the enduring effect of the promises or oath of God to the next generation if they would believe the divine word. The new, believing generation would not forfeit their right to participate in these gifts in the promise of God.

In like manner, therefore, our Lord will roll away the current reproach of the hostile pagan world on evangelicalism if we meet God's condition of belief and trust in his specific interventions on behalf of his bride, the Church!

The Effect of the Celebration of the Passover on God's Provision – 5:10–12

It was now time for that special renewal of Israel, for this time was not disconnected from the other times in the past and the future. Israel had been carefully instructed in Exodus 12 that the sacrificial lamb was to be chosen on the tenth day of the first month and the Passover meal was to be held on the evening of the fourteenth day. The Israelites crossed the Jordan on the tenth day of the first month (4:19) and celebrated the Passover meal on the fourteenth day (5:10). Accordingly, the very first Passover meal in Canaan was likewise to be a "memorial" (Exodus 12:14) of that night forty years ago when God delivered Israel with his mighty hand from slavery in Egypt to this new beginning that opened a whole new future for them (Exodus 12:29).

There are six great recorded Passover festivals in the Old Testament, each of which marked a significant turning-point that separated the past from the future. The first Passover was the one celebrated in Egypt, marking the end of slavery and the beginning of forty years trekking through the desert from Goshen to Gilgal in Canaan (Exodus 12:27–29). The second Passover came exactly one year later and was held at Mount Sinai, just when the covenant teaching had been completed and the long journey from Sinai to the plains of Moab got underway (Numbers 9:5). The third is the one mentioned as the first Passover in the land of Canaan (Joshua 5:10). It separated the years of desert travel from the years of living in their own land. Then, for the next 300 years of the monarchy, there is no record of a Passover festival until the fourth Passover was celebrated by King Hezekiah, marking the end of a long period of disobedience and the commencement of the reform movement in Israel (2 Chronicles 30). The fifth Passover was led by King Josiah in 622 B.C.E., marking the beginning of a national revival that came at the time of the collapse of the Assyrian Empire (2 Kings 23:21–23). The sixth and final Passover took place in 515 B.C.E., when Zerubbabel was governor and Joshua was High Priest in Jerusalem and the Second Temple was completed. This marked the end of the Babylonian exile, and the high hopes for a coming messianic age.

Israel, the text proudly states, ate some of the produce of the land of Canaan on the very next day after Passover (5:11). A new age had begun. We read three times (5:11–12) that they were no longer eating manna but the produce of the land. This would have been the time at the beginning of barley harvest. The Feast of Unleavened Bread began also on that very day after Passover (5:11).

The Effect of Yeshua's Appearance on Joshua – 5:13–15

Joshua was walking alone near Jericho—as close as he dared go without his army, I suppose—wondering what the next step would be. No divine command had yet come to him, but when he lifted up his eyes, there, right before him, was a person brandishing a sword. It wasn't one of his soldiers; they wouldn't have been there without being ordered to. Instead of retreating, Joshua took aggressive action and challenged this person by demanding, "Are you for us or for our enemies?" (5:13c). This man responded: "Neither … but as commander of the army of the LORD I have come" (v. 14). His "nay" answer meant he was neither friend nor foe; he had come as the commander and captain not of a human army, but of the armies of God. This signaled to Joshua that this man was none other than the "Angel of the Covenant," the same angel who had come to Abraham under the Oak of Mamre, apparently the same one who had wrestled with Jacob at Peniel near these very banks of the Jordan. Joshua now faced none other than the pre-incarnate Messiah, the Lord himself.

As soon as Joshua realized to whom he was talking, he fell face-down in full reverence. In many ways, this was what he had been waiting for, for he needed instructions on what he was to do next. The captain of the Lord's armies had an answer: Joshua could begin by "taking off [his] sandals" (Exodus 3:5–6). What a comfort this must have been for Joshua and his army, who were about to carry out a military conflict to have the presence and the promise of the God of gods on their side! The ultimate responsibility for the huge conflict that would now ensue would not rest on Joshua's shoulders, or on any of the twelve tribes; no, the battle belonged to our Lord, and so did the victory.

Conclusions

1. We must prepare our hearts and our whole being for meeting with the Lord who is sovereign over all. How can we do this?
2. Outward ceremonies, signs, seals, and liturgies mean very little, if anything, if not accompanied by the inward works of God.
3. History, and we ourselves, are visibly changed by the interventions of God. Often our Lord has asked us to use various memorials to help us to recall all that he has done for us. These become memorials of times when God has specially met with us.
4. God stands ready to intersect our lives, our times, and our situations as he shows up as the captain of the armies of heaven and earth.
5. Will we make the necessary heart and working actions to prepare for his working in our lives? This may include, at times, taking off our shoes and showing full regard for the fact that as we meet him, we are often standing on holy ground.

Questions for Thought or Discussion

1. How is the Passover connected in its meaning and significance to the Lord's Supper or the Eucharist?
2. How may we use the rite of circumcision in our modern times? How does the New Testament refer to this command of God?
3. How is the Jordan River best described spiritually in our modern era? Does it refer to passing over "death," as some hymns teach?
4. How was the preparation to cross the Jordan like our call in our day for a revival of our congregations, homes and nation?

Lesson 5

Conquering What Is Devoted to the Lord

Joshua 6:1–27

The city of Jericho was at this time locked down so tightly that no one went in or out of the city (6:1). It was at this point that the Lord told Joshua he had delivered over the city of Jericho into his hands, along with its king and its fighting men (v. 2). The Lord told Joshua to march the army of Israel around the city of Jericho for the next six days, once each day. God gave Joshua very specific instructions:

> "Have seven priests carry trumpets of rams' horns in front of the ark. On the seventh day, march around the city seven times, with the priests blowing the trumpets. When you hear them sound a long blast on the trumpets, have the whole army give a loud shout; then the wall of the city will collapse and the army will go up, everyone straight in." (6:4–5)

On the seventh day of circling Jericho, the march was to continue this day for seven times of circling, which would begin early in the morning and continue late that day, for at the signal sent by Joshua, the air was to be rent with the shouts of the people and the blare of the trumpets all sounding at once (vv. 4b–5). On this seventh trip around the city, the wall of Jericho would collapse so that each man in the army would be able to go straight up from his position in the line of march into the city (v. 5). Let us see just what happened because of all this preparation.

By Counting on the Lord's Presence – 6:6–15

There is little doubt that the Ark of the Covenant held center-stage in this first city attacked in the land of Canaan, for it appears no less than ten times in this chapter. The Ark was the symbol of the Lord's real and powerful presence as Israel moved forward in an endeavor they had been involved in for the first time in their recent triumphs over the Transjordanian kings Sihon and Og. Here was a terrific lesson for Israel and for all times: No one goes forth in the service of our Lord on their own wits and strength. In fact, the resources of our Lord's infinite power are available for all service offered and rendered to our God. Even where our Lord sent out his disciples to witness to the truth of the gospel for him globally, his strong affirmation was, "Lo, I am with you always, even to the end of the world." That was the declaration that motivated William Carey, one of the earliest missionaries to India, in 1792. His response began the modern missions movement. Carey was heckled for promoting such a venture of bringing the gospel to the heathen, for his fellow believers said, "When God pleases to covert the heathen, he will do it without your aid or mine." But Carey is said to have answered these naysayers by citing Matthew 28:20, adding this wonderful retort: "If this text is not written for us but for Jesus' disciples alone, then they must have lived awfully long lives—in fact, until the end of the world!" Carey went forth nevertheless, and God blessed his ministry immensely! Therefore, our faith in the powerful and reassuring presence and magnificent word of God and the promise of his presence will result, as it did for Joshua in his victory over Jericho, just as the Lord acted in later history to remove the "mountain" that stood blocking Zerubbabel in Zechariah 4:7. Zerubbabel found out that it was "not by might, nor by power, but by [God's] Spirit" that God's marvelous works were accomplished. That is what Israel was about to demonstrate and what God's people are to realize in all their confrontations with the workers of iniquity!

Joshua had strictly instructed the people of Israel not to give a war cry, nor to shout during any of the six days of circling Jericho. They were to say nothing until Joshua gave the signal to shout and yell aloud to the glory of God (v. 10). This, then, became the other half of the lesson that comes from the siege of Jericho: A great deal of the work of God is unseen and goes on without our involvement. The people said and contributed nothing for the six days of preparation for the city's fall and merely shouted on the seventh day!

Just as Gideon's battle cry, which came during the time of the Judges, was a victory cry for the people as they smashed the pitchers concealing their torches and shouted, "A sword for the LORD and for Gideon!" (Judges 7:20), so too it was likewise a cry celebrating God's ascending to reign triumphant over all resistance of all enemies (see Psalm 47). Often God's work goes on in silence for years, then suddenly it all comes to light in a single day. Thus, in a similar way the Reformation of the Church dragged on for centuries throughout the Middle Ages with martyrdoms of men like John Huss and Jerome of Prague, John Wycliffe of England and the suppression of the Lollards of Scotland. But when this work was finally fulfilled, it was one mammoth triumph of the grace of God and his Church.

The sounding of the trumpets made of rams' horns was a warning to those in Jericho, and the whole land of Canaan, that God was about to act. Isaiah 18:3 warned that "all the inhabitants of the world" would "hear" when that final trumpet in the last day will be sounded. Amos 3:6 says, "When a trumpet is blown in a city, do not the people tremble?" I was only a youngster during the World War II when suddenly in the evening the air-raid sirens would blare, and all lights had to be shut off and curtains and shades pulled down, so no light escaped, thereby making it difficult for the enemy planes to spot their targets.

But all of that will be only a fraction of the impact seen here; it will be nothing in comparison to the trumpets that will announce the Lord's coming. There will also be seven trumpets that will signal the events of the last days, as clearly announced in Revelation 8:7, 8, 10, 12; 9:1, 13, each marking one disaster after another that will hit this old earth! But in that day when the seventh trumpet finally sounds forth, it will proclaim that "the kingdom of this world has become the kingdom of our Lord and of his Christ, and he shall reign forever and ever" (Revelation 11:15).

In 2 Chronicles 13:12–16, the chronicler used the events of Joshua 6 as a model for his description of King Rehoboam of Judah's battle against Israel's King Jeroboam. He said: "'Behold, God is with us at our head and his priests with their battle trumpets to sound the call to battle.' ... And they cried out to the LORD, and the priests blew the trumpets. ... And when the men of Judah shouted, God defeated Jeroboam ... and God gave them into their hands."

Israel circled Jericho for six days, but things were different on the seventh day. On that day the final destruction of Jericho took place!

By Entering Into the Lord's Victory – 6:16–21

The reference to the "seventh day" raises the question: Did Joshua break the Sabbath principle of doing work on that day? But if it wasn't on the Sabbath that the march around the city began and ended, then it must have been on one of the six days of marching. Some try to cover those six days by declaring that the solemn act of silently carrying the Ark around Jericho was an act of worship, and thus the labor of those days, if one happened to be a Sabbath, was justified. But the Bible is silent about any activities that may have fallen on the Sabbath!

The conquest of not only Jericho but all of Canaan involved much "waiting" and "resting" for the Lord to arise from his place and come to give Israel the victory in each case. Psalm 44:3 echoes that sentiment:

Israel did not get the land as a possession by their own sword, neither did their own arm save them: but [the LORD's] own right hand and arm, and the light of [his] face [got it], because [he] gave favor to them.

Jericho was known as the "Moon City," while Beth-Shemesh was called "Sun City." Jericho remained "tightly closed up," for they were afraid of the Israelites (6:1). The people of Jericho had heard enough about Israel's crossing of the Red Sea, their conquest of kings Sihon and Og, and their crossing of the Jordan to frighten them into a panic!

What happened to Jericho, however, had a much wider effect in Canaan, for it struck fear into the hearts of all the kings and cities in Canaan (9:3, 10:1). This procedure and this pattern of effects seemed to follow all of Israel's conquest of the land (10:28, 30). It was God who was fighting their battles!

Of course, in Scripture there had been what we might call antecedents to what happened to this doomed city, for such would be true of Cain (Genesis 4:1–7), Nimrod (Gen. 10:9–11), Babel (Gen. 11:4), the five cities of the plain (Gen. 19:4–20), Nineveh (Nahum 3:1), Tyre (Ezekiel 26:17, 19) and Babylon (Jeremiah 50:23; Isaiah 13:19–20, 47:10–11). All these cities suffered a severe collapse and destruction.

When a long blast on the trumpets and a great shout came in the Jericho battle, the wall suddenly collapsed. What all had thought was impregnable and invincible came down at the command of God. The fact that Jericho's walls collapsed was a symbol of God's day of judgment "against every fortified wall" around every city that thought they were impervious to such an assault (Isaiah 2:15). The prophet Ezekiel used the fallen walls of Jericho as his paradigm for all the cities of the world, in that final struggle when "every wall shall tumble to the ground" (Ezekiel 38:20). Even the writer of the book of Hebrews taught that the walls of Jericho fell before the power of God (11:30).

By Distancing Ourselves From All That Is Unholy – 6:22–27

After the walls came down, Joshua gave the orders that the two men who had spied out the land should go into the prostitute's house to bring her out as the two men had pledged on an oath to her. This the men did.

Rahab, of course, had an enormous impact on the history of the God's people. Eventually she married Salmon (Matthew 1:5), a prince from the prestigious tribe of Judah, and became David's great-grandmother and thus an ancestor of sorts to the Messiah. But a host of other women impacted the future of Christianity as well. For example, St. Augustine's mother Monica tearfully prayed for her son to turn from his rebellious ways, which he did. He profoundly affected Christian theology. Then there is Anthusa, the mother of Chrysostom who was used of God to declare Christianity as a legal religion. Add to this list the names of Nonna, the mother of Gregory of Nazianzen; Macrina and Emmelia, the mother and grandmother of Basil the Great and Gregory of Nyssa; their sister, who was also named Macrina; Theosebia, the wife of Gregory; and Marallina, the sister of Ambrose.[1] All these women were important because they shared in a remarkable renown that set high-water marks for the faith given to us from the prophets and apostles.

We do not know how well Rahab was accepted into the community of Israel. Was she given a chilly reception and regarded as a reprobate and an outsider because of her prior occupation? We do not know.

Jericho was placed under the ban (Hebrew *herem*). When an object, person or place is devoted to destruction, those so devoted are strictly off-limits to the people of God. Thus, a city that has turned away from God must be "utterly destroyed" (Deuteronomy 13:12–14). Everything put under the *herem* must come back to God

---

[1] This list of names was suggested by William Garden Blaikie, *The Book of Joshua* (Minneapolis: Klock & Klock Christian Publishers, 1978), 158.

who owns all. To save for oneself a memento from such a site that has been devoted to God is to be personally polluted and infected by such a curse (Deuteronomy 7:26; Joshua 6:18–19).

So strong was such a ban placed on a site that Jericho was never to be rebuilt again (6:26). Later, however, in direct disobedience, a man named Hiel rebuilt Jericho (6:26). In violation of God's direct warning, this man from Bethel laid the foundation of Jericho at the expense of the death of his oldest son Abiram. He further violated God's decree when he set the gates to this city, and his youngest son Segub died (1 Kings 16:34).

Conclusions

1. It is the mighty presence of God that turns ordinary problems into extraordinary acts of God.
2. The long blast of the trumpet is God's warning that his judgment will come one day upon this earth.
3. God is never absent, even when we do not see anything happening after we have toiled and prayed. He is still present as he had promised even though we cannot see him for the moment.
4. All walls of all cities will collapse before the appearing of our great God and Savior in that future day.
5. In no way should we touch or take as a souvenir of the event, place or person anything that is doomed or set for destruction by God.
6. The names of women have held a special place in the work of God over the ages and should not be forgotten.

Questions for Thought or Discussion

1. What must the average Israelite have thought when they were told that the way to conquer Jericho was to march around once every day for six days and then on the seventh day seven times? What sort of military strategy was that?

2. What do you think was the purpose for the silence on the march of the first six days? We mortals like to think we contributed something to bring about the final effect, so how much of the victory of Jericho could Israel claim in this instance?

3. In what ways did God insist that Jericho be a hallmark for all the conquests that were to come?

4. How did the use of the ban contribute to this city that marked the model for all the other cities that would be attacked in the future?

5. Why did God place an eternal curse on the city so that the man who tried to restore the city would be the object of the curse?

Lesson 6

Falling Into the Hands of an Angry God

Joshua 7:1–26

After such great success following the crossing of the Jordan and the conquest of Jericho, one would think that Israel was beginning to get the hang of how to go about conquering the land. However, chapter seven instead begins by asserting that "the Israelites were unfaithful in regard to the devoted things … so the LORD's anger burned against [them]" (7:1). It will turn out that the sin that had been committed was by one individual, a man by the name of Achan, but it was imputed to all the people of Israel, because in this situation they were regarded as one unified people. Suddenly they were faced with sinners in the hands of an angry God!

Such a summarizing statement recalls a famous sermon given by Jonathan Edwards (1703–58) in the First Great Awakening, "Sinners in the Hands of an Angry God." In this sermon, Edwards referred to Revelation 19:15, where this phrase is found: "the winepress of the fury of the wrath of God Almighty." Edwards explained the words of Revelation 19:15:

> "The words are exceedingly terrible. If it had only been said, 'the wrath of God," the words would have implied that which is infinitely dreadful: but it is "the fierceness and wrath of God.' The fury of God! The fierceness of Jehovah! O how dreadful must that be! Who can utter or conceive what such expressions carry in them?"

Edwards knew the anger of God was against our transgressions, but he also knew the blessedness of heaven as well, which he described in his lesser-known sermon "Heaven Is a World of

Love." But as John Piper expressed it, the truth is this: "Those who have the largest hearts for heaven shudder most deeply at the horrors of hell."

No person in the act of sinning can be sure that the consequences of his sin will stop with himself, for in this case Achan sinned, and as a result wrath fell on the whole congregation. He had taken some of the spoils of the battle, and all Israel had been strictly warned not to do so. All was to be dedicated to the Lord and destroyed.

There Are Public Effects of Our Individual Sins – 7:1–5

It seems Achan was not some poverty-stricken person in Israel, for no doubt he owned oxen for plowing his fields, sheep for cash income, and donkeys for transportation, for he came from a prominent family of Judah (see Genesis 38:12–26). Thus, his motive for taking these spoils from the loot in Jericho, despite clear instructions not to do so, was not because of poverty or the lack of any goods, but a desire for luxury. So, he took the Babylonian garment, the bar of gold, and two hundred shekels of silver and hid them in his tent (7:21).

The Lord had warned Israel to "keep away from the devoted things, so that [they] will not bring about [their] own destruction by taking any one of them. Otherwise [they] will make the camp of Israel liable to destruction and bring trouble on it" (6:18). Accordingly, Israel had been warned that when one person sinned by taking any of the devoted things, trouble would come to the whole group. However, the sad truth was, "the Israelites were unfaithful in regard to the devoted things" (7:1).

Unfortunately, when Joshua sent only two or three thousand men from Jericho to attack the small town of Ai, which is near Beth-aven, i.e., Bethel, "for only a few people lived there" (v. 3d), they were surprisingly and swiftly routed by the men of Ai, and thirty-six of them were killed as the rest of the Israelites were chased from the city gate (v. 5a). "At this, the hearts of the people [of Israel] melted with fear and became like water" (v. 5c). Israel had lost decisively. Something was terribly wrong.

There Are Despairing Perplexities That Come to Our Leaders Under God's Wrath (7:6–9)

As a result, Joshua tore his clothes and fell face-down to the ground before the Ark of the Lord and remained in this position until evening. The elders of Israel followed suit as they also sprinkled dust on their heads (v. 6). Meanwhile, Joshua moaned,

> "Alas, Sovereign LORD, why did you ever bring this people across the Jordan to deliver us into the hands of the Amorites to destroy us? If only we had been content to stay on the other side of the Jordan! Pardon your servant, LORD. What can I say now that Israel has been routed by its enemies? The Canaanites and the other people of the country will hear about this and they will surround us and wipe out our name from the earth. What then will you do for your own great name?" (7:7–9)

Joshua and the elders were shocked by the wholly unexpected outcome of this second battle in the land of Canaan. Some modern interpreters charge Joshua with unbelief, thinking his complaint was akin to the murmuring of the congregation resorted to in their days in the wilderness. But Joshua's were not words of unbelief; they were words of despair and of not knowing what to do in such a circumstance. Making one's complaint known to God is not the same thing as complaining *about* God or his actions. The great commentator Matthew Henry correctly commented on Joshua: "We cannot urge a better plea than this, 'Lord, what wilt thou do for thy great name?'" It was the honor of God's great name that had upset Joshua. If Israel perished, it would not reflect as poorly on them as it would on God's great name.

There Is a Full Disclosure of Private Sins in the Revelation of God – 7:10–15

As we have seen already in 7:1, there is an interplay between the one and the many, for when Achan sinned, all Israel sinned (7:11). That is why the Lord commanded Joshua, "Stand up! What are you doing down on your face?" (v. 10). It is a fact that all Israel had sinned, for now the Lord would show Joshua why the small town of Ai had trounced them so badly in the attack on their village (v. 12). It is impossible to stand before one's enemy when there is sin in the camp or the congregation! God cannot bless when there is hidden sin in our midst! Only twenty-first-century believers will feel this is an unfair verdict on the whole group. Our Lord cannot be with us or the whole group unless the one who committed the sin of disobedience is likewise handed over to destruction for his sin (v. 12b).

The process for locating the culprit must begin with each person in the congregation "consecrating themselves" (v. 13a). This was to be done in preparation for the next day, when the culprit who had sinned and what he stole would be revealed. There was no chance Israel could stand before her enemies until the devoted things were removed from that person (v. 13d). When Achan stole these items, God had forbidden Israel to take, Israel had forfeited the presence of God in their midst. No wonder, then, that they were so sorely trounced by such a tiny village. When we are unwilling to purge evil from our midst in those difficult moments of costly congregational discipline, we forfeit the presence of God and operate without the evidence of his power. Admittedly, some are too punitive and overly insensitive in their application of such discipline, so that there is no regard for the person, just for the judgment of that person.

But most congregations today err on the other side, being too lax, and rarely if ever use the ministry of church discipline to bring sinful members who repent back into the fold. The Church must heed the words of 1 Corinthians 5:1–13 and 2 Thessalonians 3:6–15. Too often we prefer the route of tolerance of men, rather than the praise and presence of God. 1 Corinthians 5:5 urges us to "hand [that offending person] over to Satan [if there is no confession and repentance of sin] so that the sinful nature may be destroyed and the spirit of that offender may be saved in the day of our LORD."

There Is Awful Severity Against Sin in God's Wrath – 7:16–26

Early the next morning Joshua had all Israel come forward, each represented according to their tribes. The tribe of Judah came forward, and the family of Zerah was picked out by lot. Then the families of Zerah stepped forward and the family of Zimri was chosen. Joshua had the family of Zimri come forward man by man, and Achan, the son of Karmi, was identified as the culprit (vv. 16–18).

At this point, Joshua said to Achan, "My son, give glory to the LORD, the God of Israel, and honor him. Tell me what you have done; do not hide it from me" (v. 19). Joshua did not speak in a paternalistic or hypocritical way; he spoke compassionately all the while dealing firmly with the sin.

We can sort of feel for Achan; I doubt he got any sleep the night before the confrontation, knowing the Sovereign Lord would point to him the next day. We can even imagine his heart beating violently as the procedure unfolded. As his tribe was singled out, his stomach must have rolled into a knot. Finally, when the chosen lot turned to his family and his name was called out in public, everything must have turned to one blur of momentary darkness for him. He had been caught red-handed; he had sinned and caused the death of thirty-six men. And in so doing, so had all Israel sinned as well.

Joshua sent messengers immediately to investigate Achan's tent, and there were the items (v. 22). They were gathered and taken to Joshua and the waiting nation. Then they were spread out before Joshua and the whole nation and the Lord. Clearly to steal something that was not one's own, especially an item devoted to the Lord, was to steal from the Lord himself!

The severity of the judgment that followed was also an index to the enormity of the sin. This was not only stealing but stealing directly from God things that had been devoted to him. Joshua and all Israel took Achan, the silver, the robe, the gold bar, his sons, his daughters, his cattle, donkeys and sheep, his tent and all that he had out to the Valley of Achor (meaning "valley of trouble"). Joshua plaintively asked Achan, "Why have you brought this trouble on us? The LORD will bring trouble on you today" (v. 25). Then the Israelites stoned Achan to death.

"Over Achan's body they piled a huge heap of rocks, which remain there until this day. Then it was that the LORD turned from his fierce anger and the name of that place in still to this day called the Valley of Achor" (v. 26).

Conclusions

1. Hidden sin is not truly hidden, for it is open to the eyes of the Lord.
2. God cannot bless the group (whether a business, a congregation, a state, or a nation) to which I belong when there is unconfessed sin found in my life.
3. In Joshua 7–8, there are four stone monuments set up in the land as reminders to times when God has acted on our behalf, or when we have failed our Lord: (1) the pile of stones reminding us of Achan's sin in the Valley of Achor, (2) a pile of stones at the site of Ai ("ruin"), (3) a stone altar of reconciliation between God and man in 8:30–31, and (4) the monumental stones that show God's Covenant is of primary importance to righteousness in the land (8:32).
4. The severity of the judgment is an index of the enormity of the sin in God's eyes.

5. Just as we cannot treat cancer with placebo pills, neither can sin be treated with "cheap grace" or by pretending it doesn't exist.

Questions for Thought or Discussion

1. Do you think Achan thought he could get away with violating God's command since he came from one of the finer families in Israel?
2. The one who sinned brought the whole nation under the condemnation of sin. Did this mean in every case that the children could be put to death for the sins of their parents and vice-versa?
3. Who was responsible for the death of the thirty-six men who lost their lives in the battle with Ai?
4. Why was it necessary for the nation to consecrate themselves in preparation for the choosing of the right man by lot the next day?

Lesson 7

Upholding the Righteousness of God

Joshua 8:1–35

With the fall of Jericho, Joshua now sent out spies to get the lay of the land on the next Canaanite fortification to be conquered, which was the site of Ai, "near Beth-aven" (7:2). No miraculous elements were involved in the conquest of the biblical town of Ai, today often identified as Khirbet et-Tell. It has had many significant excavations recently, but it seems to lack any evidence of occupation between 2400 and 1200 B.C.E., which overlaps with the conquest era of 1400 B.C.E. This, then, cannot be our site of Ai!

However, more-recent excavators have argued for a better identification of Bethel as Bireh, just 550 yards south of the twelfth Roman mile-marker from Jerusalem, as mentioned by Eusebius (ca. 269–339 C.E.); as the site of Bethel. This seems a better fix on where Ai was; if that identification is correct, the town of Ai can be equated with Khirbet Nisya, a small site east of Bireh. This suggested site of Ai has all the geographical and topographical markers cited in Scripture: a valley to the north (see 7:2; 8:10–13), which goes down into the Wadi Suweinit, which descends to Jericho; Jebel el-Tawil, a hill on the far side; and a ridge on the west side that presented a perfect place for an ambush without being seen from either Bireh or within Khirbet Nisya. So far, though, Khirbet Nisya has not provided any building remains attributable to the Middle Bronze Age. Biblical archaeologist Brian G. Wood has suggested another possible site for Ai—Khirbet el-Maqatir, whose excavations have shown it to be a site that also fits the biblical evidence of its surroundings and shows a Late Bronze I fortress that was destroyed by fire (Joshua 8:28).

The chronology and geography are difficult to unravel, but we may be close to figuring out where Ai was located. Chapter 8 also seems to describe two ambush forces sent out on two different days (vv. 3–9, 10–13), but such a conclusion is not in accord with the Lord's instructions in v. 2. It is best to see only one ambush group and only one night of attack involved in Ai's capture. In that case, then, 8:11–13 used a flashback as indicated by the syntax of verses 11 and 14. Verse 11 begins with a disjunctive circumstantial construction that introduces a retrospective account in vv. 11–13. More of this will be discussed in our study of this lesson.

In Our Lord's Reassurances and Directions – 8:1–2, 18

Our Lord's encouraging word to us, as it was to Israel's army even as they were sent to attack Ai, was this: "Do not be afraid; do not be discouraged." That word of encouragement was often on God's lips as seen elsewhere, such as Deuteronomy 31:6, "Be strong and courageous." The reason Israel was told to be strong and resist any waves of fear was also given in this passage: "For I have delivered into your hands the king of Ai, his people, his city, and his land. You shall do with Ai and its king as you did to Jericho and its king" (8:1d). Another reason why God's people should abandon any anxious thoughts about what could happen in their conquest of Ai, and not be overcome by discouragement, was because "the LORD [our] God goes with us; he will never leave us nor forsake us" (Deuteronomy 31:6d).

That was the same word of encouragement God gave Moses to give to the twelve spies, those he would send out to survey the land of Canaan in Deuteronomy 1:21, "Do not be afraid or discouraged." To help those in Israel who might have become faint of heart, they were told, "Do not be afraid of them; remember well what the LORD your God did to Pharaoh and to all Egypt" (Deuteronomy 7:18). The psalmist's reminder for all of them was the same good word as well:

"The LORD is my light and my salvation. ... Whom then shall I fear?" (Psalm 27:1)

After Achan's sin had been dealt with, God's gave very detailed instructions, including even when the timing of the battle was to occur (8:18). Interestingly, both verses 1–2 and 18 head up two major sections in this chapter, yet both also give strong reassurances and courageous directions for the path the army was to take in its conquest of the land.

Unlike the clear directive in the conquest of Jericho, in the taking of Ai the people were allowed to take the spoils of victory for themselves (8:2). This precedent is seen in Deuteronomy 2:34–35. When the Lord's priority is recognized and satisfied, he shares the spoils with his people. Our Lord did not wish to impoverish his people; he wanted to help them and bless them. But what caused the people of Israel and some of us toward impoverishment was covetousness, which caused Israel and some of us to lose sight of God's generosity, goodness, and provisions. It is not God but the tempter who wants us to focus on God's restrictions and make us feel like God's priorities are unwarranted and harshly imposed limitations. However, godliness with contentment, taught the Apostle Paul, is great gain.

In Our Lord's Gifts and Victories – 8:3–17, 19–29

Joshua, acting on the instructions the Lord had given him, gave detailed plans for attacking Ai (8:4–8). As discussed earlier, 8:11–13 appears to be a flashback that goes over the same ground as vv. 3 and 10. In v. 3, Joshua states his decision to move out against Ai, but it is only in v. 10, i.e., the next morning, when the army actually moves out for battle. However, that previous night Joshua had sent out a portion of his army to set an ambush "behind the city" (8:2, 4). The next morning, with a residual force of Israelites, he pretended they were once again about to be vanquished; Israel's army fled Ai, leaving the town unguarded while its army chased Joshua and his troops. Joshua and company fled, seemingly in defeat, while the ambush that had been prepositioned at an observation spot between Bethel and Ai (8:9) waited for Joshua's signal. When they saw him hold out his javelin toward Ai, the ambushers rushed to the city, captured it and "set it on fire" (8:8).

Too late to remedy the situation, the small army of Ai, upon looking back over their shoulders and seeing smoke coming from Ai, realized they were trapped. The city was wide-open for the invaders to burn and loot. Joshua 8:12 says there were 5000 involved in the ambush. The number of those in the ambush is sometimes confused with the 30,000 in verse 3, but such a large number would not be the right size for an ambush—that is, 30,000 is likely the *total* number of men involved in the operation. Thus, 25,000 would have provided logistical support for the 5000 ambushers, who took the city unopposed as part of the plan to conquer Ai.

Again, the prearranged signal between the ambush group and the main contingency of the army was that when Joshua held out his javelin toward Ai, the men in the ambush were to rise from their hiding place and take control of the abandoned town. The term for Joshua's weapon, translated as "javelin" (Hebrew *kidon*), was not the usual word for a "spear" (Hebrew *hanit*); it might have been a short sword of some type. Whatever its name, Joshua kept it outstretched until the entire population of Ai had been killed (vv. 25–26).

As the battle progressed, when the men of Ai looked back and saw the smoke rising from the town, they saw "they had no chance to escape in any direction" (v. 20). Just how the ambush saw this signal, since they were behind the city of Ai, is not described, but it could easily have been relayed to the ambushers by others who were in better positions to see the signal. The men of Ai were caught between Joshua's troops coming out of the burning town of Ai and Joshua's main contingency now facing them (vv. 21–22). Israel cut down men of Ai, leaving no survivors or fugitives. Some 12,000 Aiite men and women fell that day (v. 25). Everything that lived in Ai was destroyed.

The site of this battle overlooked the Arabah (v. 14), which is the name of the great rift valley in which Jericho, the Jordan River, and the Dead Sea are located. So, the battle headed down toward this geological depression, moving in an easterly direction. The "desert," which was further ahead of the way the battle was going, is more properly "the way of the wilderness," and it may have been the name of a particular road or escape route (v. 15).

The body of the king of Ai was impaled on a pole and left there until evening (v. 29). Joshua further instructed that the body should be taken down at the evening hour and thrown down at the entrance of the city gate, with a huge pile of rocks placed over it, "which remains to this day" (v. 29). The king's body was taken down at sunset to show Israel obeyed the law given in Deuteronomy 21:22—that a corpse should not remain exposed overnight. The king's fate was the same as Achan's, for the words are identical: "They erected over him a large pile of stones [which is there] until this day." This action makes the point that God would not favor his own people when they had blatantly disobeyed him any more than he would favor those Canaanites who also disobeyed his law!

The question always arises at this point, "Was God just in such actions against the king of Ai and his town?" The answer is yes, for the Lord had patiently waited some 400 years (Genesis 15:16) for the Amorites and Canaanites to repent, but they instead worked continually on filling up the cup of iniquity. Rather than repenting and finding new life in the Living God, the people of the land became notoriously wicked as they practiced idolatry, bestiality, and even polluted the land with child sacrifice (2 Kings 16:3, 21:6), magic, necromancy, and murder of God's prophets, along with all sorts of sexual perversion (2 Kings 23:7, 21:6; Jeremiah 26:20–23). When the cup of sin and iniquity became full, God stepped in with his judgment as he did in Noah's day (Gen. 6:5), and he will yet step in one more day as Sovereign over the whole earth (Revelation 11:16).

In Our Lord's Reminders of His Blessings and Curses – 8:30–35

Students of the book of Joshua are greatly perplexed by the place that this final section of chapter 8 has in our Bibles. A quick look at a map of Israel shows that Mounts Ebal and Gerizim, located in the plain of Shechem, are quite a distance from Bethel and Ai. How could Joshua have gone so far through the central part of Canaan, presumably still hostile territory for Israel, without noting any conflicts, battles, or wars to clear out that land? Therefore, many have come to suspect this passage was meant to be placed elsewhere, textually, in the book of Joshua.

But it may well have been that the people of Shechem were friendly, not hostile, to Israel. Or was Shechem actually hostile but didn't dare challenge Israel in light of their clear victory over kings Sihon and Og, and the cities of Jericho and Ai? Whatever the case, the book does not describe Joshua and Israel taking any of the cities in the central area of Canaan such as Aphek, Taanach, and Megiddo, though it is later noted in Joshua that these sites were also defeated. If so, Israel likely *did* fight these other cities, but the battles were not included in the book of Joshua.

It may be that the Israelites were now the victorious army controlling the central ridge highway that went northward over the top of the mountain range toward Shechem through the center of the country. They traveled for some twenty miles until they could see two mountains over to their left, Ebal and Gerizim. Ebal stood more to the north, and Gerizim stood to the south, with the city of Shechem (meaning the "shoulder") between them. Mount Ebal was where Moses had commanded the Israelites build an altar when they entered the land (Deuteronomy 27:4–5). But these mountains were also significant also for another reason. Mount Ebal and Mount Gerizim were the places on which the twelve tribes were to stand— six tribes on each mountain for pronouncing, perhaps antiphonally, one blessing followed by one curse from the law of Moses. The blessings were given on one mountain and the curses of the covenant on the other mountain, to renew the covenant as they entered the land (Deut. 11:26–32; 27:2–13; 31:9–12).

But even further back in history, Shechem was where Abram (later called Abraham) received the promise upon entering the land for the first time (Gen. 12:6–7). It was also at this place where Jacob had returned safely after being away from the land of Canaan for a long time after stealing his brother's birthright (Gen. 33:18–20) and where he too had received the divine promise of the land, as he left Canaan for that extended period (Gen 28:11–13).

At the instructions from the Lord and his servant Moses (v. 31), Joshua built on Mount Ebal an altar to the Lord. It seems significant that it was not built on Mount Gerizim, the mount of blessing. Perhaps this was a reminder to the people that they were not going to be perfect and would need an altar to confess their sin before the word of God could take up lodging in their hearts. This altar was composed of uncut stones on which no iron tool was to be used, as Moses specified. It also had no steps, just a ramp leading up to it as was also specified in the Book of the Law. On some of the flat-plastered covered stones, Joshua wrote a copy of the teaching of Moses. Moses had instructed (Deuteronomy 27:1–4, 8) that uncut stones were to be used to step up the altar. The unique plastered-over ones had a kind of calcium solution on which the word of God could be copied. Mount Ebal and Mount Gerizim were about a mile and a half apart at the summits, but only 500 feet apart at their base. Gerizim reached to 2895 feet and Ebal 3077 feet above sea level. This meant Gerizim stood 800 feet above the valley and Ebal about 1000 feet. Both names, Ebal and Gerizim, mean "barren." From the top of both mountains, most of the Promised Land can be seen. Also, these mountains are a place where natural amplification is present; a person could stand either on the peak or sides of these mountains and hear what was said or read on the other mountain. Moreover,

God had marked out Mount Gerizim to be the mountain from which the blessings were read, and the taller mountain, Ebal, was designated as the mount of warning, or the place from which the curses were recited. The readings would alternate, a blessing and then a curse.

In the late 1970s, an Israeli archaeologist embarked on a surveying campaign of several places in Israel that were important to the narrative of the Bible. Adam Zertal (1936–2015) of Haifa University was the archaeologist who was to survey the tribe of Manasseh's hill country; Israel Finkelstein of Tel Aviv University was to survey Ephraim's hill country.

On April 6, 1980, Zertal, an archaeology professor, came across a site known as "el-Burnat" ("The Hat" in Arabic, named for its appearance), a large pile of rocks on the northeastern slope of Mt. Ebal, some 60 meters from the summit. It had two occupation levels: Level II he dated 1300–1270 B.C.E., and a younger Level I he dated 1250 B.C.E. But there was an Egyptian scarab found there from Pharaoh Tuthmosis III, which would permit a 1406 B.C.E. date for Joshua's Altar.[1] Some archaeologists agree, noting that Israel had crossed the Jordan River precisely 40 years to the day since leaving Egypt on Nisan 14 in 1446 B.C.E. Then he defeated Jericho and Ai.

The place where Joshua built an altar for burnt offerings goes back to the days when Abram came to this same spot upon first entering the land. There is some manuscript confusion over the sites named Ebal and Gerizim because of the long-standing dispute between the Samaritans and Jewish people. But the icing on the cake for the discovery on "The Hat" (see 8:32) is that Joshua instructed them to write on the stones a copy of the teaching Moses had given them. The excavators found, buried inside the altar, plaster-covered flat stones with biblical references!

---

[1] Adam Zertal, "Has Joshua's Altar Been Found on Mt. Ebal?" *Biblical Archaeology Review* 11.1 (Jan/Feb 1985): 26–43.

This site of Shechem is also significant for being near the well where the Samaritan woman met Yeshua (while the disciples were in Shechem to get groceries). Jacob's Well lies between Mounts Ebal and Gerizim. It was this woman who no doubt turned and pointed to Mount Gerizim and said, "Our fathers worshiped on this mountain" (John 4:20), but Yeshua did not take the options she offered, i.e., of Israel's worshiping either on Mount Gerizim or on the mountain in Jerusalem. No, he pointed to himself as the proper object of worship. This woman could not come to God by the law, for Yeshua alone was the way, the truth and the life. He was the Savior of the world, and she appears to have put her trust in him.

The people of one half of the tribes were to stand in front of Mount Gerizim, and the other half of the nation was to stand in front of Mount Ebal, just as Moses had commanded they were to do as they entered the land of Canaan (v. 33c). Afterward, Joshua read all the words of the law (v. 34). Joshua did not omit one word from all that Moses had written in the law (v. 35). All this took place at Jacob's Well in Shechem.

Conclusions

1. When the Lord says he is our ever-present help in a time of trouble, we should never be afraid or discouraged. We need to turn to him in times of trouble.
2. God is in charge of everything including the timing of events as well.
3. Even though God is very patient, waiting 400 years for Canaan's cup of iniquity to be filled up, yet even that patience and opportunity to repent has limits, as the Amorites and Canaanites finally discovered.
4. God's gracious covenant has both blessings and curses assigned for different sets of responses.

5. If only Achan had waited and not disobeyed in stealing and hiding what was dedicated to the Lord at Jericho, he could have had all he wanted of the loot of Ai.

Questions for Thought or Discussion

1. What do you make of the similarities or differences between Moses holding his hands up in prayer as Joshua fought the enemy in Exodus 17 and Joshua holding the javelin in his hand to vindicate that God was in the right and had no shadow of right or wrong in him (8:18, 26)?
2. How can believers be strong and courageous in facing problems in life? Why is fear of the face of the enemy so self-defeating?
3. When sin is dealt with, as in the case of Achan, God is free to grant us victory. What illustrations of such a sequence could you cite for history or your own life?
4. What is the theology behind the demand of *herem* and giving to God the first-fruits of our successes as it was in Jericho? Why should we devote gold, silver, iron and the like to God to be put in his house at the start of major campaigns?

Lesson 8

Failing to Inquire of the Lord

Joshua 9:1–27

The site of the city of Gibeon is now called today el-Jib, a town 6.5 miles northwest of Jerusalem, on the main road for going cross-country, stretching east to west from the central highlands to the coastal plain. Gibeon is presently occupied, so only a minimal number of excavations has been able to be conducted on that site. However, it did show a strong wall from the Early Iron Age (Iron I) and an elaborate water system with an underground storage system capable of holding 25,000 gallons of wine in jars. The city was surrounded by vineyards and fertile fields; an agricultural area extended six-tenths of a mile to the south to the site known as Nebi Samwil ("the prophet Samuel").

Gibeon was one of the royal cities that was in league with other towns on this east-west road: Beeroth (1.25 miles south of Gibeon), Chephirah and Kiriath-Jearim (about 6 miles west and south of Gibeon). This quadrangle of towns controlled the critically important east-west road that crossed the country from the seacoast to the Jordan Valley at Jericho by way of Bethel and Ai. These four cities, however, unlike the other cities in Canaan, did not have kings to rule over them but "elders" (9:11). Did this leadership pattern indicate these towns were in a vassal relationship to the king of Jerusalem? If so, this would explain why he became so upset when the towns made an alliance with Israel. But this has not been substantiated.

The Gibeonite quadrangle was highly contested territory, for the Philistines sort of assumed it was part of their territory. In fact, they established a chariot camp at the city of Micmash; thus, this east-west road was thought to belong to Philistia by this hostile force. The Gibeonites were known as "Hivites," which may mean they were newcomers to the land of Canaan from areas up north. Later, for reasons unknown, the Gibeonites fell into disfavor with King Saul, so he tried to destroy them and drive them out of the land despite the covenant they had made with Joshua during the days of the conquest of Canaan. Could it be that the Gibeonite in David's army was one of David's heroes (1 Chronicles 12:2, 4), who fled from Saul to David's refuge at the same time when Abiathar the priest also left Saul (1 Samuel 22:19–23)? Was this why Saul was angry with the Gibeonites? The city of Beeroth received the same purge Gibeon did, which may explain why two men from Beeroth assassinated Saul's son, Ish-bosheth (2 Samuel 4:2–3). Did Saul sense that the Gibeonites were beginning to side with David as he was losing control of them?

The elders of the quadrangle must have decided to sever their ties with the Jebusite king of Jerusalem, if the elders of Gibeon had been at all submissive to him, and therefore they abandoned their alliance to the king of Jebus (i.e., Jerusalem) on the condition that they could make an alliance with the Israelites, who were about to conquer them as Israel left Gilgal! Let us study this narrative more closely to get as many details as we can.

We Will Experience the Results of Not Having the Wisdom of God – 9:1–15

Israel had been clearly warned, of course, not to make a treaty with any of the population of Canaan (9:24), for they were to be separate from them. That word had been given by Moses in Exodus 23:31–33:

> "I will establish your borders from the Red Sea to the Mediterranean Sea, and from the desert to the Euphrates River. I will give into your hands the people who live in the land, and you

will drive them out before you. Do not make a covenant with them or with their gods. Do not let them live in your land or they will cause you to sin against me, because the worship of their gods will certainly be a snare to you."

Moses had repeated the same word in Exodus 34:12–14:

"Be careful not to make a treaty with those who are living in the land where you are going, or they will be a snare among you. Break down their altars, smash their sacred stones and cut down their Asherah poles. Do not worship any other god, for the LORD, whose name is Jealous, is a jealous God."

The Gibeonites' ruse can be found in 9:3–4, 12–13. The delegation arrived at Israel's camp in Gilgal on donkeys loaded with stale provisions, made up of "worn-out sacks, old wineskins that were cracked and mended." These lying Gibeonites' sandals were "worn and patched" and their "clothes were old." They claimed to have traveled from a "distant land" (9:6, 9, 13), but they were lying through their teeth! These guys were so good at their deceit that they could have won an Academy Award for their acting! The Gibeonites did indeed look like a grubby, dusty, motley crew from far away. Things seemed to be going quite well for their play-acting, for success was attending their way so far. It looked like they were going to pull off their charade big-time. In the meantime, "all the kings west of the Jordan [had] heard about" [the victories Israel had been having], i.e., "the kings in the hill country, in the western foothills, and along the entire coast of the Mediterranean Sea as far as Lebanon (meaning all the kings of the Hittites, Amorites, Canaanites, Perizzites, Hivites, and Jebusites" (9:1). All of them came to wage war against Joshua and Israel (9:2)—except the Hivites of Gibeon! They had a different plan to save their necks!

iviteivitWhat helped them was that Joshua had forgotten the lesson Moses had taught him when they were attacked by the Amorites; Moses kept praying, with Aaron and Hur holding up his hands in constant prayer, as Joshua victoriously led the troops. What he was now forgetting was that the tide of battle rises and falls in exact rhythm with the rise and fall of Moses' arms and hands in prayer! Most deceptive of all was the testimony the Gibeonites gave in 9:9–11. They piously recited this sort of litany:

> "Your servants have come from a very distant country because of the fame of the LORD your God. For we have heard reports of him: all that he did in Egypt, and all that he did to the two kings of the Amorites east of the Jordan—Sihon king of Heshbon, and Og king of Bashan, who reigned in Ashtaroth. And our elders and all those living in our country said to us, 'Take provisions for your journey; go and meet them and say to them, "We are your servants; make a treaty with us."'"

No one, including Joshua, remembered to ask God whether the story they were hearing was true, and whether they should make a treaty with these Hivites. God's wisdom was available; they just didn't ask for it! The Hivites put on an Oscar-worthy performance, but if Israel's leadership was to be effective, they had to steel themselves against such attacks from the enemy. Furthermore, Proverbs 3:5–7 urged both them and us, "Trust in the LORD with all [our] heart and lean not on our own understanding. In all [our] ways [we must] acknowledge him and he will direct our paths. [We should] not be wise in [our] own eyes; [we must] fear the LORD and turn away from evil."

We Will Diminish the Honor and Glory of God – 9:16–21

Three days after Israel made the treaty with the deceptive Gibeonites, the Israelites heard that the Hivites were their close neighbors, living just a short distance from Jerusalem (9:16). So, Israel set out to visit these four cities (v. 17), but they did not attack them, because they had sworn it on an oath. Not much could be done now that a treaty had been concluded; yes, even though the whole assembly grumbled against the leaders (v. 18c), Israel had given her word. The leaders could only weakly answer, "We have given them our oath by the LORD, the God of Israel, and we cannot touch them now (v. 19). So, the Hivites would remain there on that east-west road on the ridge by the grace of God!

Joshua and his elders refused to blemish the Lord's high and holy name. Such leadership also refused to be stampeded by the cries of the populace or by the failures of its leaders. They would confess to God they had sinned and needed his forgiveness. At least from to a worldly point of view, some could argue the Gibeonites had gotten this treaty and oath under false pretenses, and thus the promise didn't have to be honored. But thanks be to God, the leaders reasoned the opposite way, for to break an oath made to God, even though it had been obtained wrongfully, would be to demean his holy name and dishonor him. Israel held the name of God as a name that was most sacred and holy. The honor of God's name takes precedence over every other consideration.

We Must Cast Ourselves on The Grace of God – 9:22–27

Joshua did, however, summon the Gibeonites and asked them directly, "Why did you deceive us by saying, 'We live a long way from you, while actually you live near us?'" (v. 22) Apparently, Joshua did not wait for an answer, for in some ways the response was rather obvious! But he did go on to state this: "You are now under a curse: You will never be released from service as woodcutters and water carriers for the house of my God" (v. 23).

Finally, the Gibeonites answered Joshua,

"Your servants were clearly told how the LORD your God had commanded his servant Moses to give you the whole land and to wipe out all its inhabitants from before you. So, we feared for our lives because of you, and that is why we did this." (v. 24)

That admission on their part was amazing, for they, without having access to the teaching of Scripture by any of their leaders, or to written word of God, still had a very-clear picture of what Moses had said. Amazing! God had given the whole land over to his people Israel, and all the present inhabitants were to be wiped out—and they knew it! This was exactly what Rahab had testified that she and her people in Jericho had heard as well (2:10). These Gibeonites were ready to do whatever role Joshua and the elders should set for them, for they realized what they had done was wrong, but it had also saved them from being wiped out by Israel's army (9:25).

The Gibeonites never again give any evidence of siding with the Hivites in the rest of the biblical history, even though they were blood-related. Instead, as ordered by Joshua, they did become hewers of wood and drawers and carriers of water for the assembly of the people and for the needs of the altar of the Lord (v. 27).

Gibeon later became one of the cities where David and the Levites would place the tabernacle some 400 years later (1 Chronicles 16:39, 21:29). In Nehemiah's day, the Gibeonites were among those who worked along with the Israelites on rebuilding the wall around Jerusalem, so they seem to have identified with Israel and pitched in to help them.

In application, we need to observe that despite our heritage as Gentiles, and our own tendency to sin by lying and deceiving as the Gibeonites did, by God's grace, we too can still become part of the people of God. If the Gibeonites could find "rest" among his people, so now can all who wish to be a part of the people of God, including the Gentiles, find that same "rest" and the blessing of salvation. We too have heard of all God has done for his people Israel, so let nothing hold back any believers in our day as well for magnifying the works of our God.

Conclusions

1. How often have we as believers failed to inquire first from the Lord our directions for life's journey? Trusting in our own instincts and our own wits is not the way for us as believers to live.
2. To be sure, Joshua properly asked for real evidence that these people were from as far away as they claimed, but he had been also taught by Moses and God's word to check with God as well. In his failure to do so, he really was tricked and outfoxed by these smooth-talkers.
3. These Hivites were foreigners and Gentiles, yet amazingly they still were not without the basic facts of the story of the promises made to Israel about possessing the land or God's acts of salvation.
4. These Gibeonites also knew that it was not proper to lie to get their way, but they thought the circumstances would allow it.

Questions for Thought or Discussion

1. Why did Israel not remember what Moses had so frequently taught them about not making treaties and covenants with the Canaanites and Amorites? How does Proverbs 3:5–6 figure into this discussion?
2. Do you think there is enough evidence in the Scripture to say that some, or even a good number, of these Hivites became believers? How does their case of understanding the biblical story compare with the case of Rahab of Jericho, or even the actions of the people of Nineveh from Jonah's preaching?
3. How do you suppose the Gibeonites heard all that God had done for Israel if there were no Bibles, translations, or missionaries back then?
4. In what sense was hewing of wood and drawing and carrying water an occupation that could be glorifying to God?

5. What did the Gibeonites think was going to happen after the Israelites would learn that they were actually very close neighbors whom God had told them to wipe out? What made them think the Israelites might go easy on them?

Lesson 9

Watching God Fight for His People in the Southern Campaign

Joshua 10:1–43

O ur Scripture begins with King Adoni-Zedek of Jerusalem being exceedingly alarmed over the fact that the strategic central plateau of the land of Canaan was now owned by Joshua and the people of Israel because of their conquests (10:1–2). He could see that Joshua and his men under God had taken the central territory to the east, i.e., the area of Jericho and Ai. He was even more disturbed that Joshua had made a peace treaty with the four cities in the quadrangle in the center of that plateau and westward. In doing so, Joshua had cut the country in half and successfully driven a wedge between the north and the south parts of Canaan, thereby isolating them from helping or communicating with each other. It was a bold plan.

In fact, Gibeon was viewed as an important city and was "like one of the royal cities," one that was larger than Ai, and its men were known to be good fighters (v. 2). So Adoni-Zedek, king of Jerusalem, appealed to four other southern kings to come up with him to "attack Gibeon, because it [and the other three cities] has made peace with Joshua and the Israelites" (v. 4). That is how Joshua's southern campaign began, and it sets the stage for our investigation of this spectacular chapter.

That We Maintain Our Principles – 10:1–8

The king of Jerusalem wanted to smash the Gibeonite quadrangle for selling out to Israel by making a quick peace-treaty with them, so he sent for his four kingly cronies to help him liquidate these four

Gibeonite towns. In turn, the Gibeonites quickly sent word to Joshua at his camp in Gilgal to come to their rescue and repel the attack of these five southern kings (vv. 6–7), for Israel and Gibeon had a peace treaty between them. At first such a request from the men of Gibeon seemed the height of chutzpah—after all, they had been spared defeat mainly by tricking Joshua into believing their location was a long way off beyond Canaan to the north.

But the Lord instructed Joshua that in light of the covenant they had made with Israel, she was to go to the defense of these otherwise-tricky Gibeonites. The Lord assured Joshua that he should not fear this southern axis: "I have given them into your hand. Not one of them will be able to withstand you" (vv. 8–9). The latter part of this assurance had been spoken before (1:5). So, Joshua and his men marched all night long—likely for some 20 miles, on terrain 3300 feet above the level of Gilgal, and all in the darkness—to reach Gibeon by early morning to spring a surprise attack against the five southern kings who had come to smash Gibeon.

To review the geography, Gibeon is on the central east-west road known as "the way of Beth-Horon," a road that was most heavily traveled from Jerusalem to Aijalon (meaning "deer-field") in the west. Chephirah was about five miles west of Gibeon on a spur of the plateau. Kiriath-Jearim was about two miles south of Chephirah and about six miles southwest of Gibeon. The modern-day location of Beeroth is not known for certain.

The five southern cities that had already arrived to attack Gibeon were Jerusalem, Hebron, Jarmuth, Lachish, and Eglon (10:3). Later, some other kings faced Joshua, and they and their cities were also subsequently defeated: Azekah, Beth-Horon, Makkedah, Libnah, and Debir (10:10, 29, 38).

It is time to make this spiritual point: If our conscience is clear, we will find we are able to face enormous trials with the help that comes from our Lord. Moreover, Proverbs 11:3 reminds us: "The integrity of the upright will guide them."

That We Depend on God for Our Help – 10:8–15

It is rather striking that Joshua and the Lord worked together in their rescue mission of the Gibeonites. Joshua responded immediately to the call from these foreigners in the hill country. Then the Lord announced he had already blessed the expedition with a sure victory (v. 8). Part of Joshua's success against those attacking the quadrangle was the psychological advantage Joshua had in conducting a pre-dawn attack in the partial darkness of the hour. This advantage was heightened by the Lord's sending a violent storm with thunder, hail, and lightning. God promised to fight for Israel just as he fought for her at the Red Sea (Exodus 14:14). And so he did! The storm tracked precisely with the route the five kings had chosen.

After Joshua and his army had thoroughly defeated the five kings at Gibeon by their early-morning surprise attack, and especially after having marched the rugged uphill landscape all night for 20 miles from Gilgal, Joshua and Israel chased the kings on the road leading to Beth-Horon and continued to cut the enemy down all the way to Azekah (vv. 10–11). Meanwhile, the Lord pursued the enemy and hurled large hailstones on the five kings and their armies, "and more of them died from the hail than were killed by the swords of the Israelites" (v. 11b). Too often Yeshua is depicted as only being tender and kind. This hardly fits the picture of the Lord as Warrior in situations such as this one. We need to reintroduce into our catechism the question and theology of Psalm 24, "Who is the King of Glory?" Answer: "The LORD strong and mighty, the LORD mighty in battle!" (Psalm 24:8) Our Lord is the One who is Faithful and True, who sits on the white horse "judging and making war" in righteousness (Revelation 19:11–16). This is no fuzzy, warm, soft God who cannot stand up against all evil. He is a Warrior of enormous power!

The depiction of God as a great Warrior is set forth in vv. 10–11. Note these five verbs: "The LORD *threw* them into confusion ... *defeated* them completely ... *pursued* them ... *cut* them down ... and *hurled* large hailstones down on them." Regrettably, the NIV, RSV, and *Today's English Version* make Israel the subject of three of the five verbs, but the ASV, *New American Standard Bible*, and *The Jerusalem Bible* correctly make "the LORD" the subject of all five of these verbs.

This description of the battle that continued that day was one that emphasized especially the miracle of prayer, for this is the emphasis of the text. Joshua commanded on the authority of heaven: "Sun, stand still over Gibeon, and you, moon, over the Valley of Aijalon!" (10:12) Thus his prayer must have come in the predawn darkness just before the battle broke out. The battle began just as the sun was rising over Gibeon and the moon was setting over the Valley of Aijalon according to the words of Joshua's prayer. Such a juxtaposition occurs only during a full moon, which would also have given the troops the maximum amount of nighttime illumination as they moved topographically upward from Gilgal.

The intention of Joshua's prayer was that both the sun and the moon should "be silent" or "dumb," which is the more-accurate translation of the Hebrew word *daman*, and a better rendering than "stand still." So, the first part of verse 13 should be translated, "The sun refrained from shining and the moon ceased [to shine]." The Hebrew word rendered to "cease" comes from `amad, meaning "to stand." Verse 14: "There has never been a day like it before or since, a day when the LORD listened to a human being. Surely the LORD was fighting for Israel"—indeed, he had heard Joshua's prayer. Moreover, the words Joshua quoted are found in the Book of Jashar, which is not a part of the inspired Scripture. It was, however, was mentioned 400 years later in the time of David; thus, even though it was not an inspired text, it did evidence some popularity. In conclusion, then, rather than speaking of this as the "Long Day of

Joshua," it would be more accurately called the "Long *Night* of Joshua," for the Lord stayed with Israel's army from the march the night before from Gilgal, and all through the next day, which remained overcast or dark from the violent hailstorm that took the same track from Gibeon on then onwards to the south and west to Azekah, as Joshua and his men were moving to catch the fleeing five kings and their armies. Given the presence of violent thunder and giant hailstones, it would seem that the shining is what had ceased, and the darkness came with the storm.

That We Are Willing to Get Involved – 10:16–27

Thus far, the Lord God himself has been very much involved in routing the enemy, defeating them, pursuing them, cutting them down, and even hurling deadly hailstones at them. The five kings who instigated all these actions retreated and fled for safety to a cave at Makkedah (v. 16). When Joshua learned that the kings had abandoned their posts as leaders to hide in a cave, he ordered that large rocks be used to seal the cave mouth, and that a guard be posted to guard it while Israel continued to close in on the remnant of the enemy from the rear, making sure they did not reach their cities (vv. 17–19). It was time now for Joshua and his troops to finish the blitzkrieg the Lord had so beautifully instituted and carried out against the southern campaign of the five kings.

Only a few survivors left from the five-king army able to reach all the way to their fortified cities (v. 20). Amazingly, the entire Israelite army returned safely to Joshua, and not a soul dared utter a word of condemnation against the Israelites (v. 21). Joshua ordered the mouth of the cave be opened and the five renegade kings be brought to him (v. 22). These were the kings of Jerusalem, Hebron, Jarmuth, Lachish, and Eglon (v. 23). Joshua ordered the men of Israel to gather around him and behold these five royal criminals. Then he instructed his army generals to come and put their feet on the necks of the kings, which they did (v. 24). Joshua's purpose in carrying out this little ceremony was for Israel to know that the Lord had been faithful in his promise to help them and to grant Israel success in the conquest of the land. The word the Lord gave to the army was the same word he had used to encourage Joshua when he began this endeavor:

> "Do not be afraid; do not be discouraged. Be strong and courageous. This is what the LORD will do to all the enemies you are going to fight." (v. 25)

Then Joshua put all five kings to death, and he left their bodies exposed on five poles, where they remained hanging until the evening. At sunset, Joshua ordered these corpses be taken down from their poles and thrown into the cave where they had gone to hide. There they would stay forever! Joshua had boulders placed against the mouth of the cave. They were still there when this book of Joshua was written (vv. 26–27).

That We Remain Confident in the Lord's Promises – 10:28–43

On that same day Joshua took the city of Makkedah and put the city and its king under the sword (v. 28). Six more cities and their kings met the same end: Libnah, Lachish, Gezer, Eglon, Hebron, and Debir (vv. 29, 31, 33, 34, 36, 38).

Seven phrases[1] are repeated time after time in this short section:

> The "utter destruction" (*harem*) of the people – vv. 28, 35, 37, 39, 40
> Every person (*nephesh*) in it – vv. 28, 32, 35, 37, 39
> None remaining – vv. 29, 30, 33, 37, 39, 40
> Fought against – vv. 29, 31, 34, 36, 38
> Took it in battle – vv. 32, 35, 37, 39
> Smote it – vv. 28, 30, 32, 33, 35, 37, 39, 40, 41
> With the edge of the sword – vv. 28, 30, 32, 35, 39

1 This list appears in E. John Hamlin, *Joshua: Inheriting the Land* (Grand Rapids: Eerdmans, 1983), 90.

These words, which may seem harsh to many, show that our Lord had waited until the moral and spiritual breakdown of these Amorite and Canaanite cities was so steep that it was time the land should be cleansed of its idolatry and abominable practices. Thus, a *herem* was called for, i.e., an utter destruction. These nations had been given much time to repent. But since there was little or no response, the judgment had to come! The Lord did not desire that these cities and nations should perish, for he wanted all to come to repentance. But after calling and calling and seeing little or no response, the justice of God finally showed up and his long-suffering came to a close.

Conclusions

1. Israel was rebuked for failing to first inquire from God if the story the Gibeonites told them was true. Moreover, Israel was told long ago not to make a treaty or covenant with any of the people of the land of Canaan.
2. Despite Israel's disobedience, the Lord was still willing to fight for his people. What doctrine does this illustrate?
3. Israel was told to not lose heart or be afraid but to be strong and courageous, for God would be with them. How did that help them?
4. God held back the shining of the sun and the moon so that the whole southern campaign could be finished in one day.
5. The Lord is a mighty Warrior against the enemies of his people, and he will fight to deliver them.

Questions for Thought or Discussion

1. If we give our word to maintain the peace, even if it is obtained from us by deception and trickery, are we obligated to hold true to that word? What if we argue that this was time in the time of war? Would that make a difference?

2. Should Joshua have come to the defense of the Gibeonites after they got their way using trickery? Why not say that God was using the enemy to pay them back for their deception?

3. Did God stop the rotation of the earth for almost a full day in order to save Israel? Is this possible? Why argue it was just the illumination of these bodies of light that was stopped? What is the significance of the verb "be dumb" or "be silent" here?

4. Why post the five kings on poles when they are already dead? Why make the cave they hid in their final resting place? How does that help the community?

5. What was Joshua's strategy in attacking the center of the county first?

Lesson 10

The Northern Campaign by Jabin, King of Hazor, at the Waters of Merom

Joshua 11:1–12:24

The action of Joshua now switches the conquest narrative to northern Canaan as Jabin, king of Hazor, serves as the ringleader of a coalition of kings of the region of Galilee, who were bent on stopping Israel from gaining any further conquests in the land. Joshua 9:1 proleptically says the kings of the north "came together to wage war against Joshua and Israel," but this "gathering together," which specifies that the rendezvous site was "the waters of Merom" (11:5, 7; sometimes wrongly equated with Lake Hula), did not occur until after the events in Joshua 10 and 11. This coalition of armies, however, apparently was not formed until after the fall of Jericho and Ai.

Note how remarkably the Gibeonite fraud of being from the far north, and Joshua's honorable action in later coming to their defense, benefited Israel in the final arrangement of things. If Joshua, after discovering the Gibeonite ruse, had repudiated the treaty trickily made by Gibeon, or disregarded their appeal to him for help when the southern five kings attacked them for selling out to Israel, then little may have hindered Adoni-Zedek and the other southern kings from uniting with the northern kings against Joshua into one huge, formidable force! But the spectacular victory God gave to Joshua in the Plain of Gibeon, down the Pass of Beth-Horon and into the Valley of Aijalon, decimated the whole plan of the southern coalition of kings.

Hazor was called "the head of all these kingdoms" (11:1–10). Its massive site consisted of some 30 acres in what was called the

Upper City of Hazor with some 175 acres making up the Lower City, with an estimated population of 40,000. One of the main branches of the Via Maris trade route from Egypt to Syria and Mesopotamia passed near Hazor. Hazor, or Tell el-Qedah, is about ten miles north of the Sea of Galilee. Most evangelical archaeologists say Hazor was destroyed by Joshua in the Middle Bronze Age around 1430 to 1400 B.C.E.; others date its demise much later, around 1225 B.C.E.

The Opponents of the People of Israel – 11:1–5

The total number of wars of Joshua extended some five to seven years altogether. The northern contingency was subdued at the waters of Merom. Some of these northern sites, such as Madon and Akshaph, cannot be identified with any degree of certainty. The northern battles seemed to cover both Lower and Upper Galilee, and Joshua's battles involved contests with the Canaanites, Amorites, Hittites, Perizzites, and Jebusites in the hill country and the Hivites below Mount Hermon in the region of Mizpah (v. 3). The only parts of the country Joshua did not overtake were the land of Philistines to the south (now called the Gaza Strip), the coastal region of Tyre and Sidon to the north, and some small kingdoms to the northeast.

The coalition of these kings all came with their armies and a large number of horses and chariots. They were one huge host, "as numerous as the sand of the sea" (v. 4). Together these kings joined forces and made camp at the waters of Merom to fight against Israel (v. 5).

The Adequacy of God's Help – 11:6–11

This text recognizes the significance and importance of God's sovereignty in vv. 6–7. God promised to hand over all the northern nations that had assembled to attack them. Joshua and his army blazed into the enemy camp "suddenly" in a surprise attack, presumably at night. The presence of the sovereignty of God did not mean human activity or effort was unnecessary or irrelevant; they went together—the divine action and the human effort! In no sense did Joshua let go of the work of leading the troops just because God was now present; no, it meant it was time for him to grab hold and lead. God's sovereignty stirred up the confidence of all involved, but it did not call for mortals to abandon their efforts and work since God was now operating as well. Joshua attacked Jabin and his coalition of northern kings in their camp "by the waters of Merom" (v. 7). In fact, Merom might only have been an assembly point where enemy troops intended to encounter Joshua later on and possibly further south on the Plain of Esdraelon, where the chariots had a better chance of maneuvering in the flat terrain as opposed to the rocky landscape farther north!

Joshua defeated them and pursued these kings and their armies "all the way to Greater Sidon, to Misrephoth Maim, and to the Valley of Mizpah on the east, until no survivors were left. Joshua did to them as the LORD directed: He hamstrung their horses and burned their chariots" (vv. 8–9). This illustrated what Psalm 20:7 teaches, "Some boast in chariots, some in horses, but we will boast in the name of the LORD our God."

Hamstringing the enemy's horses and burning their chariots showed that Joshua and Israel would not try to imitate the culture and its implements of warfare, which no doubt were all the rage. Instead, Joshua instructed his army to make the horses they had captured useless for fighting by cutting the large tendon at the back of the knee on the hind legs. Since the chariots were generally made from wood, they too could be burnt up in the fires set by Joshua as his men overran the enemy. It's not that the Israelites were culturally backward and therefore slow to pick up on new advances in technology. On the contrary, they were more attuned to divine vigilance and the omnipotence of God than they were impressed by recent technology! When the Maker of Heaven and Earth is fighting for you, all other tactics or gadgets generally seem irrelevant!

The Model for God's Servant Joshua – 11:12–15

Joshua took all the royal cities and their kings as he put them to the sword (v. 12). However, he was careful not to burn any of these cities except Hazor, for they needed houses to live in after they had conquered the land. His faithfulness is seen in this marvelous statement: "[Joshua] left nothing undone of all that the LORD had commanded Moses" (v. 15b). This meant that what God had told Moses, so Moses had carefully commanded Joshua in the same things. It meant driving all the people in the land of Canaan out of that country, for they represented a spiritual cancer that would infect Israel if it had been left as a residual virus in the land! For example, to sample some of the commands God had given to Moses, we read this from Exodus 34:11–16…

> "Obey what I command you today. I will drive out before you the Amorites, Canaanites, Hittites, Perizzites, Hivites and Jebusites. Be careful not to make a treaty with those who live in the land where you are going, as they will be a snare among you. Break down their altars, smash their sacred stones and cut down their Asherah poles. Do not worship any other god, for the LORD, whose name is Jealous, is a jealous God. Be careful not to make a treaty with those who live in the land; for when they prostitute themselves to their gods and sacrifice to them, they will invite you and you will eat their sacrifices. And when you choose their daughters as wives for your sons and those daughters prostitute themselves to their gods, they will lead your sons to do the same."

This instruction was repeated to Moses in Numbers 33:52–54 and Deuteronomy 20:16–18. God had for hundreds of years waited for these peoples to turn in repentance back to him, but it was mostly to little or no avail, thus the divine hand of judgment had to fall on these people.

A Recap of the Whole War – 11:16–23

This section is bracketed off and therefore sort of makes up a self-contained unit that opens and closes with "So Joshua took all the land" (vv. 16, 23). The text goes on to specify exactly what "the entire land" included: the hill country, all the Negev, the whole region of Goshen, the western foothills, the Arabah, and the mountains of Israel and their foothills. This land included everything from Mount Halak, which rises from Seir to Baal Gad in the Valley of Lebanon just below Mount Hermon. Joshua captured all these territories' kings and put them to death. In fact, Joshua waged war against all these kings for a good while. Except for Gibeon, not one city made a peace treaty with him, for he took all of them in battle (v. 19). Why did he encounter such resistance? Verse 20 explains:

> It was [because] the LORD himself had hardened their hearts to wage war against Israel, so that [Joshua] might destroy them totally; exterminating them without mercy, as the LORD had commanded Moses.

Here was a clear indication that the day of grace had disappeared (Gen. 15:16), for the cup of the Canaanites' iniquity was now full and overflowing the brim. There would be no divine turning away from their persistence in their long-practiced roles in idolatrous and orgiastic worship in an array of all sorts of gods and goddesses. It was after rejecting the Lord's persistent calls to turn to him and repent that he "gave them up" and ordered the destruction of their nations. Given the history of centuries of these nations rejecting God and his grace, there is little reason we moderns should find the Lord's hardening work troubling. We are told that it is a fearful thing to fall into the hands of the Living God (Hebrews 3:12–13). Those who think they can escape such judgment in our day by fleeing to the "security" of the New Testament will find the same Lord in these pages as well! Let it be affirmed that the "hardening" of Pharaoh's heart was for the same reason God "hardened" the hearts of all these kings in Canaan: Pharaoh and these kings did not heed the signs God and long chances God had given them to repent. The Lord knew the hearts of all these leaders quite well, for it was the same state of imperviousness as was found in Pharaoh's heart: "I know that the king of Egypt will not let you go unless compelled by a mighty hand" (Exodus 3:19).

Startlingly, there is no record of any battles being fought in the land between Gibeon and Galilee, known as Ephraim. Moreover, in the list of kings captured and killed in Joshua 12:9–24, there are 28 kings mentioned who are not seen elsewhere in the Joshua narrative. Nevertheless, two rather-important ceremonies are mentioned as happening in Shechem, in Ephraim (see 8:30–35, 24:1–28). Some argue that this might be explained by the fact the Hivites, who also lived in Shechem, had an alliance with their relatives in Gibeon and therefore Joshua faced no interference from the Shechemites when he went there. We cannot say for sure.

The Conquest of Transjordania – 12:1–6

Since we have already read about the defeat of kings Sihon and Og in Transjordania, why raise the topic again? Well, for one reason, they earned a permanent place in Israel's remembrance of the works of God. They appear frequently in Israel's praises and prayers of thanksgiving to our Lord (e.g., Deuteronomy 31:4; Psalm 135:11, 136:19–20; Nehemiah 9:22).

But there is a second reason as well. The writer of Joshua was careful to maintain the unity of the people of God. Moreover, the two-and-a-half tribes who settled on the east side of the Jordan River feared the day might come when someday they would no longer be regarded as a genuine part of Israel. Thus, the writer of Joshua responded to the same fear by including these two-and-a-half tribes in the survey of the conquered territories.

Summary of the 31 Conquered Kings – 12:7–24

By gathering this list of conquered kings, Joshua has been able to show that our Lord has been faithful in all he has promised. This list also establishes the goodness of our Lord, for in so doing, Joshua has been able to show that the covenant God made with Abraham (later repeated to Isaac and Jacob; see Genesis 15:18–21) has been fulfilled in all its details, just as Psalms 105, 135 and 136 demonstrate.

As some scholars correctly note, Joshua 12 is not only a summary of the conquest up to that date, but that every one of God's victories over his enemies was always a partial portrayal of what his coming victory in the consummation of history will be like. If our Lord has been this good and this faithful in the past, he will be more than able to do the same and even more in the grand finale of all history!

Conclusions

1. The Bible warns believers not to put their trust and confidence in horses and chariots and implements of war, for our trust is in the Lord, the Maker of Heaven and Earth.
2. Despite the dominating presence of King Jabin of Hazor, who led the northern confederation of hostile cities, Joshua and Israel were empowered to take them and soundly defeat them.
3. Joshua is credited by the Lord for doing all he had commanded him to do in his northern campaign. He fully obeyed the Lord.
4. To the kings who had experienced God's grace and calling for so many centuries, God hardened their hearts so they would not remain in Israel's midst as a hindrance in their worship of the Lord. Had they turned to the Lord in belief, they could have stayed.

5. Joshua was concerned for the unity of the people of God so that those on the east side of the Jordan River might never be abandoned as part of the people of God.

Questions for Thought or Discussion

1. How would you defend the legitimacy of God's command to drive all the people of the land out of Canaan if he is a good and kind Lord?
2. Why do you think there are no battles recorded for the land of Ephraim, the region of Canaan between Gibeon and Shechem?
3. In what sense was the city of Hazor and its people seen at first to be overwhelming in the eyes of Israel? As the head of the nations in that area, what role did Hazor play in mounting the northern campaign?
4. Did Israel's act of resorting to hamstringing the enemy's horses and burning their chariots signal an indication of their culture-canceling, culture-rejecting, and backwardness in accepting modernity, when they could have modernized their future methods of attack on their enemies with new weapons?
5. Why did Israel burn to the ground only three of the sites they conquered—Jericho, Ai, and Hazor? Why not destroy all of them in the same way?

Lesson 11

An Altered Use of the
Altar at the Jordan

Joshua 22:1–34

We have come in our study to the fourth and final major section of the book of Joshua, chapters 22–24. The four sections of this book include the following messages and topics:

Joshua 1–4, Entering the Land
Joshua 5–12, Conquering the Land
Joshua 13–21, Possessing the Land
Joshua 22–24, Assembling in the Land

Since each of the final three chapters in this book begins with Joshua calling for Israel, or some important segment of it, to "assemble" (Hebrew *qara*; 22:1; 23:2; 24:1), we may therefore note that the book closes with "three assemblies" of the people of God. These assemblies could be said to be built on the important theological text of Joshua 21:43–45, which reads:

> So, the LORD gave Israel all the land he had sworn to give their ancestors, and they took possession of it and settled there. The LORD gave them rest on every side, just as he had sworn to their ancestors. Not one of their enemies withstood them; the LORD gave all their enemies into their hands. Not one of all the LORD's good promises to Israel failed; everyone was fulfilled.

The emphasis in these final three chapters is the repetition of 17 references to Israel's faithfulness to the Lord,[1] yet it is important to

---

1 The times when Israel expressed fidelity can be found in Joshua 22:5, 16, 18, 19, 25, 29, 31; and 23:6, 8, 11; 24: 14-15, 16, 18, 21, 23, 24. As listed in Dale Ralph Davis, *No Failing Words: Expositions of the Gook of Joshua* (Grand Rapids: Baker, 1988), 165.

93

note that it was a fidelity based on the Lord's prior faithfulness to them (23:5, 9–10, 14; 24:2–13, 17–18).[2] Ralph Davis observes that in this same context the text teaches: "Israel must respond in kind to [God's] unwavering faithfulness," for that nation has seen some marvelous interventions by the magnificent Lord.

A Beautiful Commendation and Exhortation – 22:1–8

Joshua called all those in the tribes of Reuben, Gad, and the half-tribe of Manasseh and began to commend them for doing all that Moses had directed. Under Joshua, over the five to seven years of conquest in the land of Palestine, these two-and-a-half tribes had not deserted their fellow tribes of Israel; they had helped carry out the mission of clearing out the Canaanites who occupied the land and who God had now ordered Israel to conquer! Joshua commended the tribes for their obedience, for the Lord their God now would give them rest on the other side of the Jordan, as he had promised (v. 4). However, these tribes were to be careful to keep the commandments and the law Moses had set forth for them: to love the Lord and walk in obedience to him by keeping all his commandments. Verse 5b: "Hold fast to him and … serve him with all your heart and with all your soul."

In vv. 6–8, Joshua charged the Reubenites, Gadites, and the half-tribe of Manasseh, who had settled on the east side of the Jordan River, to send their men into Canaan to help their brothers in the conquest of the land (1:14–15). These two-and-a-half tribes had been faithful in their promise to help their brethren to clear the land of the Canaanites living there, for "[they] had not forsaken their brothers" or their promise to do so (22:3).

It's noteworthy that Joshua commended these two-and-a-half tribes for keeping their promise to help clear the land of Canaan. Of course, the One really responsible for Israel obtaining the land of

2 Ibid.

Canaan was the Lord himself, but Joshua made it clear that these tribes had been important instruments, not to be overlooked.

Joshua concluded his farewell speech to these tribes and then sent them away to their homes on the east side of the Jordan. To the half-tribe of Manasseh, the Lord had given the land of Bashan; the other half of Manasseh was given land on the west side of the Jordan. The other two tribes of Reuben and Gad left the other nine-and-a-half tribes in the western land of Canaan at the city of Shiloh as they returned to Gilead, to the same land Moses had promised to them.

An Investigation Over the Purpose of the New Altar – 22:9–20

When the eastern two-and-a-half tribes left the assembly at Shiloh, they built an imposing altar there by the Jordan on their way home. When the rest of the Israelites heard they had built an altar on the border of Canaan at Geliloth near the Jordan on the Israelite side, they gathered at Shiloh to go to war against the two-and-a-half tribes in Transjordania for what they assumed was clear evidence of a fallen state of idolatry!

Mercifully, the Israelites first authorized Phinehas, the son of Eleazar, the priest, to go to Reuben, Gad, and the half-tribe of Manasseh along with ten men (one chief man from each of the ten tribes) to accompany him as part of an investigating committee. This delegation was authorized to ask:

> "How could you break faith with the God of Israel like this? How could you turn away from the LORD and build yourselves an altar in rebellion against him now? Up to this very day we have not cleansed ourselves from that sin, even though a plague fell on the community of the LORD! And are you now turning away for the LORD?" (22:16–18)

This delegation was to investigate what these two-and-a-half tribes were doing building an altar, for the Israelites had to learn the facts before entering into a war with them. Deuteronomy 12 comes into play here; it warned that sacrifices were only to be offered at "the place that the LORD your God will choose" (Deut. 12:5, 13–14). You can be sure that designated place was not to be at any of the places where the Canaanites had conducted offerings or orgies (Deut. 12:2–3). For Israel it meant one altar, one faith, and one people at the one place of divine appointment. Israel was not permitted to simply worship wherever the people wanted! The western tribes were concerned for a proper expression of their way of honoring God at the place he would appoint, and they feared that any infidelity by the two-and-a-half tribes would bring all twelve under judgment, for they knew any sin permitted by any of the tribes would bring judgment on all of them. If the eastern tribes rebelled against God, it would bring his wrath on the entire nation (22:18). One only needed to recall Achan's sin to recall that one man's act placed the whole congregation under divine wrath. This is a warning to the whole Church, for it is not a democracy; she lives under the kingship of Yeshua, who has put the care and protection of the whole Body under the care of its elders (Acts 20:28). The guilt of one would pass on to the whole group!

A Reasonable Explanation for the New Altar – 22:21–29

The two-and-a-half tribes, now positioned on the eastern side of the Jordan, were rightly concerned about having a godly anxiety for the proper practice and worship of the Living God (vv. 21–29). But those on the western side of the Jordan feared the newly erected altar might be an expression of infidelity and a possible turning to idolatry (vv. 13–20). But the eastern tribes affirmed that it definitely was not so! The reason for building the altar was entirely different from what they thought.

These two-and-a-half tribes affirmed by an oath that they intended no unfaithfulness in building an altar. Had that been their intention, they said, may both the Lord and the nation take vengeance on them (vv. 21–23). In truth, the reason they built the altar was simply over their anxiety that in a generation or so, those in the western tribes would look upon them as having no part in being called God's people! Without the altar as a symbol of their common identity, those in the west might claim in the future that the sons of these two-and-a-half tribes must no longer fear the Lord, for they were separate from them (v. 25). They feared the Jordan might serve as the real cause of a permanent division between the tribes. The two-and-a-half tribes were concerned about what others would think. But with the altar built as these tribes retired to their own side of the Jordan, it would be possible to point out to any who objected to the inclusion of the two-and-a-half tribes that this altar had been erected just after the conquest against such a false argument that might come from those on the western side of the Jordan. Of course, it is impossible for unity to exist between the twelve tribes when apostasy rears its ugly head; the tribes needed to take time to understand each other.

A Satisfactory Resolution – 22:30–34

It seems that when the investigating committee headed up by the high priest Phinehas and the heads of the clans of Israel heard what Reuben, Gad, and Manasseh had to say, they were completely satisfied. Phinehas addressed the Transjordanian tribes with these words:

> "Today we know that the LORD is with us, because you have not been unfaithful to the LORD in this matter. Now you have rescued the Israelites from the LORD's hand." (22:31)

Therefore, one sign that the Lord himself was indeed among them was he had kept his people from committing treachery against him, and in so doing, they had delivered Israel's people from his hand (v. 31). So, Phinehas commended the Gilead tribes and praised God for what he had done for them. His point was that Israel and the world could see the hand of God when he protected his people from his judgment! Surely it is a sign that God is in our midst when he shields us from judgment by placing us under the protection of his Son.

Fortunately for Israel and Phinehas, the need for any search-and-destroy mission was no longer as necessary, as some had thought when this altar was been discovered. When the appointed committee under Phinehas' leadership returned to Canaan, the people were glad to hear the report and that their brethren had been exonerated by the clear testimony and word of the leaders of the two-and-a-half tribes. All talk about going to war against them ceased; there was no more mention of or need for such action.

This narrative concluded with the Reubenites and the Gadites giving a special name to the altar they had built: "A Witness Between Us – that the LORD is God" (22:34; see Deuteronomy 4:32–40).

Conclusions

1. The altercation between the two-and-a-half tribes and the other nine-and-a-half tribes of Israel was significant enough to take up a whole chapter in the Bible. It raised the issue of Israel's fidelity to the Lord (22:5, 16, 18, 19, 25, 29, 31). The issue of *our* fidelity to God is just as significant! Disunity in the body of Yeshua is no small matter!

2. Joshua complimented the Reubenites, Gadites and the half-tribe of Manasseh for their faithfulness in serving for those years in Canaan until the task of conquering the land was finished, and for being careful in why they had built the altar.

3. The departure ceremony for the end of hostilities in Canaan was conducted at an assembly in Shiloh in Canaan.

4. Phinehas was sent with a team to investigate the purpose of the altar built at the border and to understand what such a structure meant.

5. The two-and-a-half tribes declared that it was far from their intentions to rebel against the Lord by building an altar for burnt offerings other than the altar of the Lord at Jerusalem (22:29).

Questions for Thought or Discussion

1. Why did Joshua commend the tribes of Reuben, Gad, and of Manasseh in 22:1–5? Is such a commendation noteworthy even to this day?
2. What did these two and a half tribes stop of Geliloth to do on their way home to Gilead? What was their purpose in doing this? How was this work misunderstood by the rest of the tribes?
3. What did Phinehas accuse these two-and-a-half tribes of doing, and what was he and the other tribes of Israel prepared to do?
4. What resolved the problem?
5. What was the name given to the altar by the two-and-a-half tribes, and how did it continue to function?

Lesson 12

Joshua: Guarding Against Apostasy

Joshua 23:1–16

J oshua 23 is the second of the last three calls for the nation of Israel to "assemble" to hear the word from the Lord. In this second call, the Lord strongly exhorted Israel to maintain fidelity (vv. 6–8, 11).

A good illustration of the warning given in this chapter can be seen in the life of Ernest Hemingway, a man of great literary talent. He was very blessed to also have as his grandparents two people known for their evangelical commitment to the Lord. Hemingway's paternal grandparents also were graduates of Wheaton College, as well as close friends of D. L. Moody. His maternal grandfather was so godly that the grandkids called him "Abba."

But despite such a heritage in the Christian faith, Hemingway left his evangelical upbringing in Oak Park, Illinois, and became part of the "Lost Generation." He said, for example:

"I live in a vacuum that is as lonely as a radio tube, when the batteries are dead and there is no current to plug into."

This very gifted man ended up taking his own life! It was a needless tragedy!

This text in Joshua gives us three *charges* that encourage us to guard us from falling away from the faith as Hemingway apparently did. It is therefore important that we pay close attention to this text.

A Charge to Keep Have I – 23:1–5

As Joshua neared the close of his life, he summoned Israel's leaders, such as elders, judges, and officials, and said, "I am very old" (v. 1). In 13:1 God told him "you are very old"; in 23:2 he comments on his age. He was very concerned that Israel remained faithful to the Lord. As noted in our previous chapter, Joshua raised this concern 17 times in chapters 22–24.[1]

Joshua carefully pointed out:

> "You yourselves have seen everything the LORD your God has done to all these nations for your sake; it was the LORD your God who fought for you. Remember how I have allotted as an inheritance for your tribes all the land of the nations that remain—between the Jordan and the Mediterranean Sea in the west. The LORD your God himself will drive them out before you, and you will take possession of their land, as the LORD your God promised you." (23:3–5)

The best defense against apostasy was, and is, to recall over and over again what God had done before. The same antidote is exactly what will help prevent us in our generation from slipping into the same type of apostasy.

Let us as believers, then, repeat all that God has done in past days for our generation. We must do this, for if we do not, then there is a strong chance that another generation will arise "who do not know the LORD, nor [will they recall] the work that he has done" (Judges 2:10).

In fact, all the days that Joshua lived, Israel served the Lord (24:3). This truth is well-stated in Psalm 78:2b–8…

> "I will utter hidden things from of old—
> things we have heard and known,
> things our ancestors have told us.
> We will not hide them from their descendants.
> We will tell the next generation the praiseworthy deeds of the LORD,
> his power, and the wonders he has done.
> He decreed statues for Jacob
> and established the law in Israel,

---

1 See Joshua 22:5, 16, 18, 19, 25, 29, 31; 23:6, 8, 11; 24:14–15, 16, 18, 21, 23, 24.

which he commanded our ancestors to teach their children,
so the next generation would know them,
even the children yet to be born,
And they in turn would tell their children.
Then they would put their trust in God
and would not forget his deeds
but would keep his commands.
They would not be like their ancestors—
a stubborn and rebellious generation,
whose hearts were not loyal to God,
whose spirits were not faithful to him.

What a beautiful summary of our joyful indebtedness to the Lord and what he has done for us all the days of our lives!

A Charge for Present Living – 23:6–13

The Joshua story is now coming to a fitting climax, for it now includes his farewell address at Shiloh and the covenant ceremony he will conduct at Shechem. As Moses had stated in his farewell some years ago: "See, I [the LORD] have set before you this day life and prosperity, death and destruction" (Deuteronomy 30:15). In this sense, then, K. H. Miskotte's observation is fairly accurate, except he doesn't seem to see the events as actual happenings:

> The Bible is essentially a narrative, a story [that] we must pass on by retelling it, and in this way, it can come about that the story may "happen," so to speak, to those who listen to it."[2]

This was indeed a time of transition once again, just as it was when Moses turned things over to Joshua. This would mark the end of one era and the beginning of another. Joshua concluded his ministry by urging Israel to keep three enormously important commands:

(1) Stay under God's word – 23:6

---

2 K. H. Miskotte, *When the Gods Are Silent* (London: Collins, 1967), 204.

(2) Cling to the Lord – 23:8
(3) Be careful to love the Lord – 23:11

Israel was warned about "turning aside" (v. 6b). They were not to associate with the people in those nations that remained among them; they were to constantly separate themselves from these nations and their practices. In fact, Exodus 23:13 had forbidden even mentioning the names of any of the false gods, for that could well be the beginning of proceeding to serving them (Amos 8:14; Zephaniah 1:5; Jeremiah 5:7, 12:16).

In the second command, Israel was to hold fast to the Lord, which brings victory. It is the same type of "cleaving" enjoined in marriages, for this is how great joy will come to the believer's life.

In the third command to love the Lord their God, there is this constant emphasis on the heart attitude of following the Lord out of a pure love for him and his name.

A Charge to Avoid the Consequences – 23:14–16

Joshua closed his final words to Israel by stressing the complete certainty of God's coming judgment if the people of Israel wandered away from God. Joshua plainly reminded those who survived him of truths that the nation of Israel knew all too well: "Not a single word [has] fallen of all the good words that the LORD your God spoke about you; the whole has come about for you; not a single word has fallen" (23:14; see 21:43–45). God had kept his side of the covenant; why had Israel slipped in her part?

But Joshua was not finished yet. He added: "And it shall be that just as all the benefits that the LORD your God promised to you have come upon you, so too he will bring upon you all the disasters until he terminates you from this good land that the LORD your God has given to you" (v. 15). That divine disaster is explained in v. 16: If Israel decided to go and serve other gods and bow down to them, the Lord's anger would burn against them, and they would be destroyed quickly and removed from the good land God gave them.

Conclusions

1. We are called in this passage to remember all that the Lord has done for us and for our redemption. This is important in order for all of us to be prepared to meet contemporary issues that often are very similar.
2. We are called upon to guard the faith found in the word of God and to love the Lord with all our heart, soul and strength.
3. Nothing brings misery to the surface faster than apostasy, and nothing brings God's blessing and goodness to believers faster than fidelity to him and his name.
4. Romans 11:22 says, "Behold the goodness and the severity of God." Both aspects of God's work and nature must be kept in mind if one is to have a balanced judgment on God's nature, character and works.
5. Staying under the teaching of and meditating on God's word will keep us from turning to the right or to the left in ethics or in spirituality.

Questions for Thought or Discussion

1. Joshua was deeply concerned that Israel would never forget all they had witnessed of the mighty victories God wrought for them. What do you think might be Joshua's estimate of evangelical Christianity today? Do we tend to forget some of our Lord's works or his nature?
2. Can you name some of the outstanding evidence where God has intervened on behalf of his people Israel? Can we list similar evidence in our day, or in your own family or life?
3. Why is it that succeeding generations do not always follow the path of commitment that the seniors who went before them evidenced?
4. What are some examples of apostasy in our day, and what should we do about such reproaches on the name of Yeshua?

5. What is the best antidote to apostasy for backslidden Christians? How relevant and useful is the call of revival in 2 Chronicles 7:14?

Lesson 13

Joshua: Choosing Today Who We Will Serve

Joshua 24:1–28

Joshua's final meeting with the people of Israel took place at Shechem.[1] There were a number of good reasons why this final assembly should take place at Shechem, even though it lay just a few miles north of Shiloh, where the tabernacle was kept at that time. As a matter of fact, Shechem had much connected with it and therefore was a good place for the final assembly, even though, as we have already announced, the tabernacle was located at that time in Shiloh.

Shechem was the first resting place where Abram pitched his tent as he entered the land in the country God had sworn to give to him. But it also was where Abram built his first altar in the country of promise. Here he received his first promise of the land. Shechem was also the place where Jacob purchased a section of the land from the Shechemites and, as noted, built an altar (Gen. 33:18–20). It was also at Shechem where Jacob buried all the idols his family had been using. We need to examine this chapter in more depth.

We Must Choose to Remember All God Has Done for Us – 24:2–13

Shechem is a most-appropriate scene for Joshua's farewell address, even though up to this point Shiloh, where the tabernacle was placed, had been the place for such gatherings (18:1). It was at

---

1 The Septuagint makes this meeting in v. 1 take place at Shiloh, then places it at Shechem in v. 25, but there is no reason to accept this confusion.

Shechem that God first promised to give to Abram the land of Canaan (Gen. 12:6–7). Possibly Joshua's farewell was delivered close to Jacob's Well, which is still operational, as I witnessed in 2019. Close by the well was the tomb of Jacob, but the well was the very place where centuries later, the New Testament Joshua, i.e., Yeshua, sat down, weary from his journey, near or at the very same well and ministered the gift of new life in him, the Messiah, to the woman of Samaria.

In Joshua's speech, recorded in this 24th chapter of his book, he began by reviewing the history of Israel, starting with the name of Abraham. Joshua had an important reason for starting with this, for he who was first called Abram, and later named Abraham, was the man who had been among the first to denounce idolatry and to urge his family to repudiate the pagan gods of the land. Thus, in his closing address to Israel, Joshua went over the key facts of the history of the nation, which began with Abraham. He pointed out that the ancestors of Israel, including Terah, the father of Abram and Nahor, had lived on the other side of the Euphrates River and they had worshiped other gods. But it was God himself who had taken Israel's father Abraham from that land and led him throughout Canaan and gave to him many descendants, including Isaac, Jacob, and Esau.

God had also assigned the hill country of Seir to Esau, but for Jacob and his family, they had been sent down to Egypt (24:2–4). That began a 400-year departure from the Land of Promise.

However, if Abraham marked the first phase of God's gracious acts to his people, the second phase involved what he had done for his people in Egypt (vv. 5–7). There he sent two leaders named Moses and Aaron. There he afflicted the Egyptians with plagues (Exodus 7–12) in order to bring the Israelites out of Egypt with his mighty hand (v. 5; Exodus 12:31–39). Then the Lord mightily delivered Israel across the Red Sea (Exodus 14–15), but he swamped Pharaoh's entire army. Here now in what remains, Joshua noted in the greater part of this historical review what God had done for the generation that was now alive in Shechem.

A third phase describing God's gracious acts involved in what he had done before Israel crossed over the Jordan River to occupy the land God had promised them. First, the victories over kings Sihon and Og are listed (v. 8; Numbers 21:21–35), and then God's marvelous thwarting of King Balak's evil desire to have the prophet Balaam, from the Upper Euphrates, pronounce a curse or hex on Israel (vv. 9–10; Numbers 22–24). This non-Israelite prophet instead repeatedly blessed Israel nonstop.

The fourth and final phase of God's gracious acts on behalf of Israel concerned God's blessings in the land of Canaan. Special emphasis is given to Israel's conquest of Jericho, but the rest of the battles are referred to only in general (vv. 11–12). What is emphasized, however, is God's gift of the land (v. 13). Verse 12 mentions that God sent the "hornet" to drive out the hostile nations occupying Canaan (Exodus 23:28). Whether this "hornet" is a metaphor for what the nations would encounter as God led Israel's troops, or if it symbolizes Pharaoh, or even if the "hornet" was the insect itself, is not clear from the sources available to us. But since the text does not refer to "hornets" (plural) but to "the hornet," the first explanation may be correct. The important fact, however, as this first section of this chapter comes to an end, is that the conquest of the land was entirely God's doing, the work of his initiatives, and the evidence of his provision.

We Must Choose to Serve the Lord – 24:14–18

Joshua addressed the assembly of Israel in vv. 14–15. He warned the people not only of their history of worshiping other gods while still in Mesopotamia, but also while still in Egypt, for Leviticus 17:7 mentioned the "goat idols" Israel sacrificed to there, and in Deuteronomy 32:16–17 the "demons" they had recently worshiped in Egypt. To both offenses, Israel added a third set of gods, "the gods of the Amorites" (24:15). Accordingly, we can see that Israel never totally rid herself of her worship of foreign deities; they keep appearing in all the days of Israel's history. This was disgusting to God and to anyone of sound mind.

Considering such past and some present idolatry, Israel was being asked to make a choice of ominous implications. Such a choice is found nowhere else in the Old Testament. Moreover, God is the One who normally did the choosing. But now Israel was being asked to decide where her loyalties would lie. Would they embrace this One true God and reject all others, as Rahab of Jericho had done? The choice was a critical one and one that could not be delayed: it was to be made "today." God had chosen and elected Israel in the past, but now Israel was being asked to choose where their loyalties and their confidence for the future would rest. Pagan gods routinely did not demand such absolute allegiance, for a heathen could adopt all or any of the gods; he or she did not need to focus and commit only to one god! So, what would Israel do that very day? Would they yield all to the Lord, or would they put their trust in false non-entities?

On the surface, the people seemed to step forward to accept Joshua's challenge to choose God alone as their God. They confessed together that it had been the Lord who brought them out of Egypt, the land of bondage and slavery, and performed all his marvelous wonders before their eyes (v. 17). Furthermore, it was the Lord who had protected them on their forty years of wandering in the wilderness and had driven out the seven nations, clearing the land for them to possess (v. 18). But was this the whole story?

We Must Choose to Count the Cost and Take Responsibility for the Covenant – 24:19–28

Joshua surprises all of us by his statement to Israel: "You are not able to serve the LORD. He is a holy God; he is a jealous God. He will not forgive your rebellion and your sins" (v. 19). This is an amazing and astounding statement, for Joshua had just urged Israel in vv. 14–15 to serve the Lord with all the fidelity of their being. But when the people said they would do just that, Joshua seemed to have turned on them and said, 'What you just promised, you are incapable of doing! God will not forgive your continual rebellion and your repeated sin!'

How can we explain what seems the most shocking statement in the Old Testament, and seems so counter to what the rest of Scripture teaches? First, let us notice that what God had stated in v. 19. It reminded the people that his forgiveness depended on whether the people had forsaken him in favor of following other deities.

The qualifiers that Joshua and Scripture place on the inability of the people to serve the Lord must be connected to two of God's defining absolutes: He is a "holy God" and a "jealous God." These two characteristics set him apart from all other gods and from his people. The pagan gods displayed raw jealously among themselves over endless petty rivalries, but God's jealousy was grounded in the fact that he would brook no competition or divided loyalties. In short, God loves his people so completely that he wants their undivided affection and commitment.

Verse 20 makes it clear, then, that Joshua's statement in v. 19 about God not forgiving his people was not intended to be an absolute and timeless principle; instead, it was a statement that made it clear that his forgiveness depended on whether the people who said they believed in him forsook him and worshipped other gods! The Lord was raising a standard against hardened disobedience and a divided heart, one that tried to have the Lord on one hand and the false gods on the other. But this was impossible with the Lord God of Israel.

Verses 21–24 deal with the people's protest (v. 21) that Joshua was mistaken when he declared them incapable of serving the Lord. But Joshua would later be proven correct; in the book of Judges, the people showed their faith in the Lord was superficial and shallow to say the least. Therefore, Joshua held the people to be witnesses against themselves. In fact, in vv. 26–27, he erected a large stone under an oak tree to function as another witness against them. The stone would act as a witness; that is, it would be as if that stone had heard all the people had resolved to do that very day and following! This is the first and only time a "covenant" is mentioned in this chapter.

George E. Mendenhall was the first scholar to identify the special "treaty structure" in Joshua 24, connecting it with parallels found in the ancient Near East, of which there are at least 57 extant examples from the ancient world.[2] Generally, the Covenant in Joshua 24 would look like this:

Preamble – 24:1–2a

Historical Prologue – 24:2b–13

Stipulations – 24:14–15, 16–25

Deposit in the House of God – 24:26

Witnesses by the People – 24:22 and by the Great Stone – 24:27

Curses and Blessings – 24:19–20

Even though Joshua 24 does not claim to be the actual *text* of the Covenant, it is a *report* of its renewal. This Covenant bound the people in a strong commitment to serve the Lord and to obey him alone and not the gods of the Canaanites, or any other false deities.

The storyline of the book of Joshua ends abruptly in verse 28 with Joshua dismissing the people so they could all go each to their own inheritance. Joshua's work had come to an end.

There is added to the book of Joshua the account of his death and burial (vv. 29–31), which is repeated with a few differences in

---

2 George Mendenhall, "Covenant Forms in Israelite Tradition," *The Biblical Archaeologist* 17.3 (1954) 50–76. See also Kenneth Kitchen, *Ancient Orient and the Old Testament* (Chicago: InterVarsity, 1966) 96–97; and Kitchen, "The Patriarchal Age: Myth or History?" *BARev*, 21.2 (1995): 48–57, 88–95.

Judges 2:6–9. Here for the first time Joshua is called "the Servant of the LORD" (v. 29), a title the book seemed careful to avoid until now—no doubt out of deference to Moses, who has been called God's "servant" 14 times in this book. Joshua was buried in the city he had asked for, Timnath Serah (see 19:50), near Mount Gaash. Joseph's bones, which had been carried out of Egypt with the Israelites when they left that land, were buried in Shechem, the land his father had bought for a hundred pieces of silver from Shechem's father Hamor (24:32). Also, the high priest Eleazar, Aaron's son, died and was buried at Gibeah, which his son Phinehas had allotted to him in the hill country of Ephraim (v. 33). Thus ended the history of Joshua.

Conclusions

1. Joshua knew his people well enough that he knew some had not yet made the choice whether they would serve God alone or one of the Canaanite idols; it was time for them to choose—that very day! They had to make up their minds!
2. Joshua knew that Israel's ancestors, including Abraham's father Terah and Terah's son Nahor, had all been worshipers of other gods. It was from such paganism they had been redeemed.
3. God had taken Abraham from the land beyond the Euphrates and had given to him descendants and the land of Canaan as he destroyed the Amorites who had previously owned the land, but who now had been driven away from that land by the strong hand of God.
4. God called Joshua and Israel to serve him (used 18 times in this chapter) and to make a choice to serve him exclusively.
5. Believers are not personally able to serve a holy and jealous God by their own efforts and willpower, for their choice to serve the Lord must be backed up and enabled by the power of a gracious and forgiving God who helps us in our weaknesses.

Questions for Thought or Discussion

1. God's choice of calling Israel to be his very means of blessing both them and the entire world had almost nothing to do with Israel's background, size, heritage, or natural gifts. It was the gift from God. How does that match our own awareness of how each of us became a child of God?

2. In your judgment, why do the final three chapters of Joshua focus on the city of Shechem rather than Shiloh, where the tabernacle was at that time, or even on Jerusalem? What made Shechem so special?

3. Why does the Lord rebuke Israel, after they seem to say, if we must choose who is our deity and Lord, then "far be from [us] to forsake the LORD to serve other gods"? Did Joshua not believe them then?

4. How can a large stone be a witness against a people, as v. 27 affirms?

5. Why do you think Joshua was not called "the servant of the LORD," as Moses had been called, until almost his last day on the job?